Dear Lord, I Think I Married The Wrong Person

~Her Story

Stories Compiled by Ayanna Lynnay

ChosenButterfly Publishing ~Books That Transform Lives~

Dear Lord, I Think I Married the Wrong Person Copyright © March 2012 By Ayanna Lynnay

Published in the United States of America by ChosenButterflyPublishing LLC

All rights reserved under International Copyright Law. Contents and/or cover may not be reproduced, distributed, or transmitted in any form or by any means or stored in a database or retrieval system, without the prior written consent of the publisher.

This book is designed to provide information and motivation to our readers. It is sold with the understanding that the publisher is not engaged to render any type of psychological, legal, or any other kind of professional advice. The content of each article is the sole expression and opinion of its author, and not necessarily that of the publisher. No warranties or guarantees are expressed or implied by the publisher's choice to include any of the content in this volume. Neither the publisher nor the individual author(s) shall be liable for any physical, psychological, emotional, financial, or commercial damages, including, but not limited to, special, incidental, consequential or other damages. Our views and rights are the same: You are responsible for your own choices, actions, and results. We reserve our right of freedom of speech, and all first names have been omitted to protect identity and all stories are truthful as each author can recall.

WWW.CB-PUBLISHING.COM

ISBN 978-0-9831637-0-1

Library of Congress Control Number: 2012932770

Second Edition Printing
Printed In the United States of America
April 2012

ChosenButterfly Publishing
P.O Box 515
Millville, NJ 08332
www.cb-publishing.com

Edited by www.extractthevision.com

Dedication

To our Lord and Savior Jesus Christ who died for our sins Past, Present and Future.

To our Families (especially our children) who have been there through the good and bad.

To our husbands and ex-husbands Thank You! Because without you this book could not have been written and valuable lessons would never have been learned.

Dear Lord, I Think I Married The Wrong Person

Our Testimonies

Introduction	7
When the Vows Break {Pastor Kim Parson}	13
UnHoly Matrimony {Evangelist Theresa Scott}	33
Two Halves Don't Equal a Whole {Rev. Dawn Williams}	49
Don't Get Got {Bobbie Clark Alexander}	67
Jesus Loves Me, This I Know {Tennie Tyler}	85
Sleeping with the Enemy {Rev. Vernora Gibbs -Chisolm}	105
A Marriage Built on Sand Cannot Stand {Ayanna Clark}	121
The Story Behind My Bling Bling {Pastor Joanne Schlicher}	143
Taking the Lord at HIS Word {Tabitha Shannon}	155
Broken to be Made Whole {Sherell Edwards}	173
Looking for Love in All The Wrong Places {DaNita Greene}	189
A Puzzle is Not Complete Without You {Genita Gentry}	201
Marriage is Not Always a Fairytale {Kendell Lenice}	213
In Spite of It All I Made It {Prophetess Amanda Williams}	231
The Love of Jesus Brought Me Out {Prophetess Tracy Davis}	247

~Each author's bio proceeds their chapter~

Introduction

You don't have to be a person of faith to know divorce is not the will or desire of God. The Bible states the Lord hates divorce (Malachi 2:16) So what would cause a Christian believer to do something that God hates? Absolutely Nothing! At least, that is what I believed until I found myself facing divorce. It is amazing how strong our convictions are until we find ourselves walking in shoes we never wanted or thought we would wear.

The Bible says *what God joins together let no man separate,* but what do you do when you know in your heart God did not join you with the person you married? I battled so hard with the idea of divorce and even found myself asking, "Is willfully marrying the wrong person the only sin that equals a death sentence?" (We did take vows of "unto death do us part")

Since the dissolution of my marriage, I have learned so many valuable lessons that I would have never learned had I not gone through what I went through. I strongly believe that we go through things in life not just for ourselves, but for others and the only way others will ever know what we have gone through is if we tell them. The purpose of this book is to do just that; To tell *our* stories.

I knew I was not the only one who said at one point in time *Dear Lord, I Think I Married the Wrong Person* so I invited others to share their testimonies as well. The testimonies you are about to read are REAL. Written by real women of God at different levels of faith who found themselves facing real issues.

Dear Lord, I Think I Married The Wrong Person

I want to tell you upfront that although all the Co-Authors are Christians this is not a theology book filled with scriptures to justify our actions. We all recognize we could have done *many* things differently, but we are willing to be transparent and share how we felt and what we learned in order for you not to have to go through some of the things we went through. It is our prayer that you would take something positive away from what we did right as well as what we did wrong.

This book is **not** pro-divorce it is pro-waiting on God. *Before* getting married, *During* the rough times in your marriage and even *After* a marriage. It has been my experience that if you don't wait on God before getting into something, you will find yourself waiting on God to get you out or to bring you in what you really need and desire. Either way you slice it, you must *wait on God and trust Him* in the midst of your waiting.

My prayer for *Singles* is: Don't compromise for *any* reason because in the end, it is never worth it. My prayer for the *Married* person who may be going through a difficult time in your marriage is: Draw closer to the Lord and follow His instructions, please don't just follow your feelings and emotions. Our feelings and emotions can cause us to walk right outside the will of God and suffer the consequences. Feelings and emotions are an indication of what we should be praying about and not necessarily how we should be acting. This is why you must draw closer to the Lord so you can obtain the strength you will need to override your emotions during this time. My prayer for those who have gone through or are going through a divorce, may you understand that while the Lord may hate divorce, He still

Dear Lord, I Think I Married The Wrong Person

loves the divorcee. Jesus died so we can have life and life more abundant. There is still life and life more abundant even after a divorce!

Father God in the name of Jesus, I Thank you for your Grace and Mercy in Jesus name!

Love and Blessings to all,

Ayanna Lynnay

Acknowledgments

I want to say Thank You to my sisters who bravely shared their testimonies to be a blessing to someone else. The fourteen of you have blessed me more than you even realize and I know your testimonies will be a blessing to others as well. I pray that the Lord will continue to use you and all that you have been through, for His glory. I pray the Lord will bless you, your families, and everything you put your hands to will prosper.

Thank you Coach Tomasso for all of your assistance and for editing our book. May the Lord open up even more doors for you to use your gift.

Pastor Kim Parsons

Is the Pastor of *Vision of Hope Ministries* located in Charlotte, North Carolina. She is the mother of five beautiful daughters. Pastor Kim Parsons (affectionately known as Pastor Kim) has over 20 years' experience as an educator and Motivational Speaker to young women and men. She also assisted her former husband in pastoring for over 25 years.

Pastor Kim obtained her Bachelor's Degree in Early Childhood and Elementary Education from Temple University in Philadelphia Pennsylvania and went on to obtain a Masters Degree in Education Administration from Cheyney University, located on the outskirts of Philadelphia. She has served as both a Teacher and Principal in the Philadelphia Public Schools and private school sector. She was the founder and CEO of a Christian school in Philadelphia, which served as an educational safe haven for many at-risk youth.

She has inspired men, women and youth at workshops, retreats, college campuses, and various platforms and events. She also has an online ministry which sends out daily email blasts entitled *"Pastor Kim's Corner of Power!"* This provides tech-savvy Christians the opportunity to read the word each day using their laptop, desktop, iPod, etc. It's a qualitative Word from the Lord in sixty seconds or less!

Throughout all her endeavors, inspiring youth and troubled families to obtain education is her passion! Her motivational scripture is: *Jeremiah 29:11 ~ "For I know the plans I have for you," declares the Lord, "plans to prosper you and not to harm you, plans to give you hope and a future."*

Pastor Kim is also the author of a journal book entitled *"Daily Affirmations for Everyday Living."* This book provides scriptures and words of encouragement in many areas of life. It also provides the reader with an opportunity to use the word of God to speak over their life each day; visualizing and creating a positive future. She truly believes we are what we say we are; which is why self-motivation through the word of God is so important in a person's life.

Her motto is: Proverbs 18:21 ~ "Life and death is in the power of the tongue, and they that love it shall eat the fruit thereof!"

Dear Lord, I Think I Married The Wrong Person

Contact Pastor Kim via

Website: www.clubvision.webs.com

Email address: ladyparsons5@gmail.com

Facebook: Pastor Kim

When the Vows Break

Honestly, I don't really think I married the wrong man; I just think we both strayed away from the will of God at different times, and it spiraled into something bigger than our faith could handle. Marriage is one of the most selfless acts anyone could enter into, yet we enter into it to receive more than we can give or are willing to give. If a person honestly feels as though they married the wrong person, then they would have to ask themselves what was the reason they got married. Was it really for love? Or was it to get away from home? Perhaps it was for security? Whatever the reason, marriage is a commitment; a commitment of two people working together. One of the reasons God ordained marriage was because it was His guarantee for Godly offspring. (Malachi 2:13-15)

I had gotten saved at the age of 14 and met my husband in the summer of the following year. I got married at the age of 19. My husband had recently gotten saved and from my understanding at that time we were no longer unequally yoked. I had been born and raised in church, so I knew that I could not marry him if he wasn't saved, however, I did go against the grain and date him. I had been witnessing to him over the years, but he did not appear to be interested, and although we talked about marriage, I told him that would not happen because he was not a Christian. Well, lo and behold, after a period of time of us dating off and on as teenagers he got saved!

Dear Lord, I Think I Married The Wrong Person

I was at Howard University, and I hadn't heard from him in months, so I called his family and they told me he had moved to Philadelphia and gave me a phone number. When I called him, he said that he had been praying about me! What? Praying about me? He stated that he had gotten saved, and we were no longer unequally yoked! Wow! There was no way I was letting him get away. My prayers had not been in vain. So we honored God by getting a license to have sex!

At that stage in our lives, a twenty-year-old and a nineteen year old, only two things mattered- serving God and having sex! Nevertheless, I know that God blessed our marriage and gave us favor beyond measure, because we honored Him in every aspect of our commitment in the beginning. We literally prayed together, discussed scriptures, encouraged one another and submitted to one another, which is why we produced babies. Any healthy relationship is going to reproduce. Businesses, churches, marriages, farms; if the ground is good, it will grow.

I can remember distinctly when I felt as though I did not want to be a part of our marriage. I was 26 years old and pregnant with my third child; my husband was pastoring and we were struggling financially and in our relationship because the pressures of life had begun to weigh heavy on us. That would not have been so bad, but we were also living according to the expectations of others within the body of Christ. Our church leaders, our congregation and our family members- *it was a lot of pressure.*

Dear Lord, I Think I Married The Wrong Person

During that time, my husband was very religious and strict. *We laugh about it now*! He didn't want me to wear pants, but I did. He didn't want me to listen to other types of music, but I did. I was not worldly, but I was in retrospect an educated individual who needed other social stimulation than children and church and there was none. I used to listen to disco to exercise; he didn't like it. I used to listen to jazz music to clean the house. I figured: how could jazz music be sinful since it had no words?! Believe it or not, we argued about it. These types of things made me think that I had married the wrong guy; when really we probably just needed a vacation with just the two of us, which we didn't take for a long time. We took vacations, but they were always with the kids or church.

One day, I was sitting on my sofa, and I started to cry because I said to myself, "I don't want to do this anymore, but I don't know how to get out of it." I was too far in. I had dropped out of college to get married and even though he agreed to support me in finishing college, after the first baby came our priorities seemingly changed. We got married in August of one year and our first baby came in August of the following year, confirming one of the two goals of our marriage! Within three years of the marriage, I had two children. I would work, get pregnant, stop working, and take a course or two at a college. Then have the baby, stop going to school, and go back to work. I was doing a lot, and even though I had a partner I felt as though I was carrying most of the weight.

At the point I felt this was not the marriage for me because I could not pursue my goals and dreams, in addition to being married and having a family with this particular person. I ignored my feelings and dreams temporarily, just continued to go through the motions of my life, and pressing in hard as Paul said, looking for that prize in Christ Jesus. (Philippians 3:14) There was no time or point in looking back, especially with kids and without an education. As we continued in our relationship, we prayed and sought both professional and unprofessional counseling.

Our once fervent prayers for one another turned into casting the devil out of each other and trying to manipulate one another through prayer and scriptures! Again, even though we are divorced, we laugh about it now. I can remember him calling me the devil (and at times I probably was), and my response was "Well you're the powerful preacher; cast the devil out of me!" On the other hand, I can recall times when we would argue all the way to church; and he would preach the word of God with power. He would literally preach me happy! At the end of the service once I went to hug him as a resolve to our confrontation and as he hugged me, he stated, "The only reason why I'm hugging you is because we're in church." How evil I thought to myself! And when we got in the car to go home, I asked him how he could preach with such power and still be so angry. He stated that one thing did not have anything to do with the other.

Men are able to compartmentalize things very well. If you think about it, the concept is biblical because a person can only reap where they sow. So, if a person only sows in their ministry and not in their marriage or children, the end result is a great ministry with an unhappy wife and messed up children who see the church world and the home world as night and day.

Dear Lord, I Think I Married The Wrong Person

I've often called my marriage a roller coaster like that old secular song. We always had high highs, and low lows. One of the things the Lord spoke to me about was refinement. I remember one day the Lord told me He was going to refine me. I had become brazen and had taken what was happening in our home life into the church because I did not know how to separate the two. Leadership meetings, the pulpit and church events became public marital wrestling matches between us. I looked up the word refined, and I remember it saying- *to use heat to get out the impurities of a thing*. I would have much rather preferred a course on refinement with a couple of books!

Another thing the Lord showed me was that He had called my husband into ministry and no one was ever going to see my husband the way I saw him. I saw him as husband first, then father, then minister. In my opinion he saw himself as minister, then father, then husband. Nevertheless, it was our job to cover one another. Unfortunately, as a young hurt couple we did not understand this and therefore, did not walk in covering each other. The church also became like our children and some of them subsequently would take sides, playing mom against pop at any given time.

One of the things, my ex-husband and I talk about when we reminisce is that we really did not have any spiritual mothers and fathers who could simultaneously relate to us and pour into us. Have you ever had someone try to give you advice, but they seemingly did not know where you were really coming from? It's almost like being in a room and everyone is speaking a foreign language, and you keep trying to explain and it seems as though people are listening but their response has nothing to do with your question or statement. That's what I call trying to pour into someone but not being able to relate. Or have you ever poured your heart out to someone and they've given you the standard set of scriptural answers? It's almost like they are using the scripture to chastise you, or make fun of you because you are supposed to be a faith believer, or they're saying, "I don't really want to hear what you're saying because I've got my own problems!" That's what I call not being able to spiritually pour into someone. (James 2:15-16)

Subsequently, we were left to ourselves with the ever popular trial and error. I know someone might say, "Well, you should have used the Bible as a guide." My response is we did, which is what helped our marriage survive as long as it did. But if you've never lived through the dynamics of family, ministry and husband and wife, most responses to these dynamics would be simply pouring in without ever being able to relate, without seeking God for an anointed response or word of encouragement.

The last thing I want to point out that the Lord showed me was even though a husband and wife come under the umbrella of family, it is a separate component of a family, in and of itself. Adam and Eve spent time together before they had children. In order to sustain a good marriage husbands and wives must spend quality time together separate and apart from their children. A sure-fire way to grow apart is to not spend any time together alone. I've known some married couples who didn't even like to be alone with each other. I don't consider that a marriage. There are a lot of people today who are technically married, but that's it.

If the relationship was ever examined or interviewed one would find that there is no fellowship, no relationship, and no one-on-one contact. There isn't even a social network! Some people have more conversation with Facebook than their spouses. That's probably the worst kind of marriage because God never called us to exist; He birthed us to have life and life more abundantly. (John 10:10).

If I had the opportunity to change anything in my relationship, I probably would have added a lot more praying, fasting, counseling and vacations. I remember praying in the church weekly, having all night prayer on Friday nights for over a year. God moved miraculously! It was so powerful. People got saved, healed and delivered. We had to put young people in their cars; they would be coming out of the church doors shouting and praising God. The police came one night because someone called and said that we were disturbing the peace. When I began to tell the police what was going on, the people began to start dancing and shouting again. The officer was shaken. He shook his head and got in his patrol car.

My problem was, with all that prayer and power, I sort of thought I had arrived and stopped, not knowing that I should have kept it going, forever. Whatever it takes to make an "A" it takes that plus more to keep an "A". I definitely would have added more fasting. People don't fast much today. Fasting has become so watered down that we ask people to give up things like television, computers, coffee and snacks. But denying the flesh is a sure way to get in touch with the Spirit. When we are able to deny our flesh, God is able to trust us. Last but not least, I would have definitely spent more time planning personal time for my husband and myself; almost forcing him to get away from the cares and responsibilities that he was under.

Seemingly much of what we learned to help save our marriage was too little, too late. The issues of life were already up past my chin and I was squirting out the waves from the storms of life trying to stay afloat. And even though we were hanging on to each other, to our children, to our ministry, to family and friends' expectations, the intensity of the storm and waves were very powerful. Finances, quality time together, family time, serving in the ministry, choir practices, weekly services, job expectations, sicknesses, church members with issues; all of these and more were waves splashing up against our lives forcing us to hold on tighter and move in closer because if one person lets go, there will be several casualties.

That's exactly what happened; someone let go. My husband stated that he wanted a divorce. I didn't believe him. We laughed and joked with each other publicly. We displayed affection in front of our children and publicly, but when we got home, we were tired and vexed. We took all of the frustrations of the day out on each other. No matter how effective I was in ministry, my husband wanted a wife. I carried our church. It was my baby. He often told me I was more of a pastor than he was because I had more patience with the sheep. We could literally be at the church working on a project together, but when we got home around ten, he wanted some form of dinner. *Well so did I!* You have to know the kind of man you marry; traditional, modern, flexible, chauvinistic, etc. He loved my ability to take control and get things done, but at the same time, his mother was a stay at home wife, something I could never be; so when we were home, unfortunately that's what he expected.

Subsequently, after a long run, we parted. He filed for divorce and moved out. Probably, the most overwhelmingly frustrating part for me was that we were both still going to the same church (after he moved out), acting like we were married. It was one of the most painful experiences of my life. Ironically, the Lord told me not to enter into ANY strife with my ex-husband during the divorce proceedings. People called me crazy. In order to keep my sanity and in order to be obedient to the Lord, I humbly walked away from a six-bedroom three and half-bathroom home, with an in-ground kidney-shaped pool; a church that I had spent over twenty-five years building; family, friends, church members, affiliate churches and a whole lot of other stuff.

This had not been our first breakup or marital struggle. The church had cried with us, prayed for us and helped restore us. But this time, it was just too difficult. It was too much pain to bear. My husband was my father, my brother, my pastor, my friend and my lover. As difficult as it was for me to stay in the relationship, I knew beyond the shadow of a doubt that my husband was not one to give up on anything! If I gambled, I would have lost because I never thought in a million years he would divorce me. But as sure as you are reading these words, the Holy Ghost sedated me through the whole process. The Holy Spirit truly gave me a peace that surpassed all understanding, even my own.

Dear Lord, I Think I Married The Wrong Person

Everyone who knew me couldn't figure me out, but God! (Philippians 4:7)

I remember going on a guided tour to the Dunns River Falls in Jamaica. A group of tourists had to hold hands and climb up a waterfall. I was reluctant so my husband and I got at the end of the line. As we began to climb I reached a point in the waterfall that was extremely slippery and the rocks could actually cut you. Also, the current of the fall was stronger. After several attempts, I could not continue so the tourist and the guide left me on the waterfall. We broke hands and they moved onward and upward. My husband stayed with me. I couldn't go back down, but I couldn't go forward. As I watched, others began to break hands so they could use both their hands to climb to survive. It became every man for himself. I'm happy to say that the tour guide came back to get me and he and my husband helped to guide me off the waterfalls. I think, to some extent, this book is being written to assist those who have been left to themselves or forgotten about or pushed to the side in the storms and waterfalls of life. *I am a living witness that you are not forgotten. Despite the struggles and setbacks, you are not forgotten.*

Today, my husband and I are divorced. Sometimes I refer to him as my ex-husband and at other times I refer to him as my husband. We were married for over thirty years so it has been both difficult and confusing. We have gone full circle, from hate, to tolerance, to friendship, to love, and back around again. I am a living witness that God will give you *peace that passes all understanding.* (Philippians 4:7) Since our divorce, I have felt abandoned, lonely, hurt, weak and not just lonely, but all alone because unfortunately when a couple divorces, friends choose sides. But the good news is I have overcome those feelings and have become filled with peace, love, joy, forgiveness and courage. I have also become empowered and unafraid to live my life to the fullest being covered and guided by God! It's a great feeling, and it brings joy thinking about it.

Since I've started a new life as a single Christian, it's been interesting to say the least. Initially I was too busy looking at myself as no longer married rather than single. I even thought I had to immediately fill the void. But thank God for Jesus. I still don't think about the actual word *single,* although I do notice single people more. My whole life was built around my marriage, my family and my church, so for a while I felt like a misfit, totally out of place. But once again, thank God I am healing, and my family is also healing. I have some old friends and some new friends, and the Lord even allowed me to start a new ministry, *Vision of Hope Ministries.* Ministry is truly my passion.

My spiritual inheritance came from my maternal grandfather, a wonderful apostolic Church of God in Christ Pentecostal Pastor! The spiritual legacy which he imparted to me could not end with me crawling in a corner somewhere feeling sorry and bitter. (Romans 11:29) His anointing was too powerful for that and his prayers along with others who prayed for me since I was a child were too powerful as well. So here I am, rejuvenated, restored, and empowered by the Holy Spirit and the Word of God! **And it's all good!** Selah! (2 Corinthians 1:20)

I do not know if I will ever re-marry. I honestly do not want to spend the rest of my life without a companion, but I don't plan on giving up a lot in order to be in a relationship, which takes me back to the beginning of this chapter! Marriage is about giving; so whatever it is that I might want out of marriage, the question is, what am I willing to give up? Due to the fact that I was married for so long, I feel as though I gave much of my life trying to please others; making sure others were happy and squeezing my own personal happiness in where ever I could fit it. Now, I don't have to do that! My children are grown, and I can just focus on God and myself and for now I'm okay with that.

In conclusion, it is my prayer that you in fact didn't marry the wrong person. I pray that God was honored in both your marital choice and your decision to get married. I pray that whatever challenges your marriage might be going through that with help and guidance in the Word of God, through counseling, and even through this book, that your marriage will not only be salvaged, but that it will take on a change and force that empowers other marriages through the challenges that you overcome.

No one knows what goes on behind closed doors except you, your family and God. My prayer is that your never be placed in an abusive situation in your marriage, physically or emotionally because God has called you to peace as a married couple. (1 Corinthians 7:15)

Here are a few hindsight guidelines for ministry couples:

- A husband and wife ought to be like chocolate milk. Once the white milk and chocolate syrup are mixed together, they are inseparable. (Mark 10:7-9) Their love for one another should be solidified before children, ministry, etc. They should cover one another and not compete against each other, (Genesis 2:24). Clinging or cleaving comes easy to a woman but a man has to work at this. Maybe that is why God pointed it out. I say this because when a lot of men marry, it is the end for them, they have proven their love and for them, as long as they provide and protect, there is nothing else to do. On the other hand for a woman, it is the beginning and she is expecting as much as she is about to give.

- A husband and wife, especially those in ministry must set aside time as a romantic couple. I cannot emphasize this enough. Women tend to feel too comfortable after marriage when it comes to romance. Men are visuals; they like beauty, they like sexy, they like romance. (Hebrews 13:4) Keep him in anticipation of you. (Song of Solomon 4:9-11) Wives are often hurt and upset when their husbands compliment other sisters in the church. It's definitely not a competition and the wife should be able to also compliment anyone her husband compliments because she is confident in whom she is and it shows.

❖ Women, keep yourself looking good and feeling good *no matter what size you are* (Ephesians 5:29) The latter part of this scripture suggests that it is a given that a person would take good care of themselves. Michelle Obama said something like *if she feels good, then the whole family benefits.* Sometimes women spend so much time pouring into others that they neglect themselves. Whether big or small, short or tall, be confident each time you step outside your door; not just comfortable, but confident; there's a difference. Don't ever start something in the courtship, like dressing nice, keeping hair and nails done, (even treating him extra special) that you are not willing to continue in the marriage. Make sure your style complements him. (1 Kings 10:4-5)

My Prayer

My prayer is that you and your spouse will walk together as a team covering one another and that you will produce Godly offspring as ordained in the book of Malachi. I pray that you learn to cover one another like never before. (1 Corinthians 7:15) He knows that you have his back, and vice versa. Just as you know beyond the shadow of a doubt whether right or wrong that God has you covered, may God give you and your spouse the strength and courage to not abandon one another, but to boldly cover one another in the face of children, family, friends and church.

Last but not least, I pray that you recognize the strength and power that a Godly marriage can have and I pray that you have the God-given wisdom to know when and how to submit to one another. But as the wife, you will have to submit more. Submission is different from subjection. Submission is a willful act based on love and trust; in the same way we submit to our Heavenly Father. Subjection is forced. So I pray again that you and your spouse will obtain divine wisdom so that you can continue to love and trust one another enough to submit to one another, in order for God's ordained purpose and plan to be fulfilled in your life. I do not just want you to be blessed; I want you to stay blessed!

This is my prayer for you in Jesus' Name ~ Amen

~Pastor Kim Parsons

Evangelist Theresa J. Scott

Was born in Philadelphia, PA. She is the 9th of 13 children. Theresa has always been a survivor. Separated from her natural family as an infant, and placed in various foster homes throughout her childhood, where she suffered various forms of abuse: sexual (molested); mental (called bad names by foster parents; made to feel like she was less than a human because she was a foster child); and physical abuse (beatings in the bathtub with extension cords; beat up by the other foster children for not participating in lesbian relationships; and beatings for no logical reason; physically and mentally abused by her second husband; raped by a "pastor" during her stay in Berlin, Germany) and the list goes on.

Although Theresa had to endure horrors that many of us cannot even imagine, it was through these dark times that she discovered the eternal light and love of God. It was, and still is, her faith that has seen her through some most difficult periods of her life. It is knowing that the Lord's promise never to leave us or forsake us is true that has sustained her.

Dear Lord, I Think I Married The Wrong Person

    Theresa received her Bachelor's of Theology degree from Bible Tabernacle College and Seminary (FL), via Heath Missions School of Theology (PA) 2000.
    Evangelist Scott was ordained an Elder in November of 2004 at Refuge of God Church Ministries, Inc., Philadelphia, and has been faithful to the call of God. She accepted her call as an Evangelist in 2010 and began the ministry Out Of A Pure Heart Ministries and has been working diligently, along with her sister Shirley, to provide clothes, shoes, socks, hats, gloves, coats and blankets to the homeless people on the streets of Philadelphia.

    Evangelist Theresa Scott is a published author of a book entitled "*An Attitude of Love: Submitting To My Husband*" (published in 2006), the host of an internet radio broadcast (blogtalkradio) and is the wife of Bishop-Elect Gerald W. Scott, Founder/Overseer of *Refuge of Hope Ministries*. They have been married for 12 years. She is a daughter, mother and grandmother; but, most importantly, she is a child and servant our Lord, Jesus Christ.

    Evangelist Theresa Scott currently attends *Strait Gate Church of Faith and Deliverance* in the Frankford section of Philadelphia – where Sheila M. Miller is the Pastor and Apostle Rich T. Miller is the Overseer.

    Evangelist Scott can be reached at:

Blogtalkradio: Evangelist Theresa Scott/Out Of A Pure Heart Ministries
Email: mrstjscott@gmail.com
facebook.com/NotWillingThatAnyShouldPerish2Peter2.9

UnHoly Matrimony

It started in 1996. I had just left California (I fled there to get away from a husband who was emotionally and physically unable to be there for me) to return to Philadelphia. Prior to me returning to Philadelphia, I was in a place in my life where I was suicidal, depressed, mad at GOD, and feeling like there was no use for me being on this earth.

My husband who I had just fled, had done something to me that he hoped would kill me… he took my children from me (through a custody battle – he had money to obtain a reputable attorney and I didn't) and did not let me know where they were.

He ignored the court order which clearly stated that he was supposed to let me know where my children were so I could call them, visit them, and send them money (when I had it), but that's another story for another book. After my husband snuck into town and took my children and ran – before the date of the court order – I had a nervous breakdown. I really wanted to die. Not to mention the person who I resided with in California told me to consider my children dead. I threatened to kill myself and some other people and as a result, I was arrested and sent to a mental facility…

In June of 1996, upon my return to Philadelphia, I was lonely, depressed and looking for "love." Not really love, but for the attention from men which I felt I deserved. I was looking for a man who was going to treat me like I had dreamed – love on me no matter what; told me that I was beautiful no matter what I looked like. A man who was handsome, patient, had money to buy me things, and would take me out to dinner. I wanted a man who could stand up and be a man in any situation. I wanted a man who understood this broken woman; this mentally and physically abused woman; this woman who had hang-ups about sex due to being raped. I wanted a man to love the little girl who was abandoned by her mother at the age of 9 months. I wanted a man who would hold me and tell me everything would be alright. Yes, I was dreaming and I was foolish enough to believe that a man, a mere man could take on all of that baggage I was carrying around.

Fast forward June 1997 and to the WRONG man I married. I had finally come to the realization that I needed to focus my attention on my spiritual life. I was unsuccessful in finding my dream man, so I figured I would do the church thing to take my mind off of not being able to "find" my prince, my knight in shining armor.

So I immersed myself in the church life. I was in ministry classes. I was in Bible Study and morning prayer faithfully. Everything the Bishop and Pastor asked me to do; I did it no matter what it was. I worked at the church like school and I thought I was growing in the LORD. And then one day it happened. The WRONG man came into the chapel where I was praying. He looked sad. I felt sorry for him. I thought, what is a handsome man like him doing in here looking all sad? He was dressed nice and was well-groomed, but he just looked so sad. So, because I thought I was so spiritual, I asked him what was wrong.

Dear Lord, I Think I Married The Wrong Person

He replied, "Nothing. I just wanted to come to prayer. I had been promising Bishop _____ that I would come so I did".

I told him that it looked like something was wrong with him and if he needed to talk, I was available. I offered to pray with him and to my surprise, he allowed me to pray for him. Dumb. Just plain ol' dumb. Ain't nobody tell me to do that. The Holy Spirit surely didn't tell me to do that. I just felt like I was so spiritual that I could help him. As I look back on this story, I realize that nobody had even helped ME!!! The broken, abused, depressed, rejected, looking for "love" in all the wrong places, woman. Yes, I was in church doing all of the church things, you know, going through the motions, but I wasn't serving *God, I was serving man and going through the motions of Church. Nobody had prayed for me to be healed from the hurt I had experienced in my life. Nobody told me that I needed to seek Jesus and worry about a man later.*

Needless to say, my invitation to pray turned into two years of hell!!! So, after I prayed with this man, he asked me if I was hungry. Smart move. I said I was and he asked me if I wanted to go and get something to eat. Of course, I said yes, and we headed off to the BUS STOP (don't laugh) and waited for the bus. Yup I said it. THE BUS. My radar should have gone off right then!!!

While we waited for the bus, we began to make small talk. He asked me about myself and I asked him about himself. He said nice things to me, one of which was that he told me I was very pretty. *Underwear alert!!! This dude is trying to get the undies already but I didn't care. He was saying the right things.*

After dinner, he offered to ride with me, home. I lived in West Philly and he lived in West Oak Lane, so that was a long ride. He'd said that he didn't want me travelling alone at night so he would ride with me to make sure nothing happened to me. WOW. Nice looking and considerate. That more than made up for him not having a car.

A few days after meeting this man, he took me to meet his mother. Now mind you, where I was living since I returned to Philadelphia was with my foster grandmother. She had warned me not to get into a relationship with ANY MAN. She told me that I needed to focus on getting a better job so I could get my own place and she also told me that I needed to focus on GOD. I wasn't trying to hear that. I was 33 and I was gonna do me. *I should have listened!!!*

Okay, so this man took me to meet his mom. She seemed nice. She acted as if she liked me. She even told her son that he picked a very nice looking woman. I was flattered. After meeting his mom he asked me if I wanted something to eat. I said yes and he ordered hoagies for all of us. After eating, I thought we were going to leave and go to his place, but then he threw a whammy on me: HE LIVED THERE WITH HIS MOM!!! HE WAS 35 living with his mom!!! OMG. But guess what? I overlooked that because his mom was cool. She was liberal. She let him live his life and she lived hers.

After we all ate and I discovered that we were not going anywhere else, he invited me to his bedroom. I was shocked and he knew it but he said we were going to watch some movies and listen to some music. His mom encouraged it because the only other television in the house was in her bedroom and she wasn't planning on entertaining me.

So, true to his word, we listened to some music and then we watched a movie. By the time the movie was put on, the horny demon exposed himself. We were on the bed – him at the foot and me at the head. My man got up, began taking off his clothes and you know the rest. His mom had been listening and said to me, "Oh, I thought you said you were a Christian. I thought you said you were a minister at your church. Why are you over here sleeping with my son?" EMBARRASSED was NOT even the right word. I thought I would just die. However, after the initial shock wore off, it was back to, well, you know.

Needless to say, I was hooked. This man said all the right things. He treated me like I was special to him. He even defended me concerning his mom. I really liked that. We were going to church together. My, my, my. How deceived I was.

As we continued to see each other, the Bishop and Pastor knew I was fornicating. They rebuked me and sat me down. By this point, I was in the choir and was an usher. I was now the leaven that leavened the whole lump. I was made a public example so that the other members would not go the same route. However, sitting me down did not faze me. Why? Because although I was embarrassed, nobody counseled this broken, abused, rejected, looking for love in all the wrong places woman. They just told me that I could not sing in the choir nor could I usher until I stopped fornicating.

Instead of stopping the fornication, it got worse. This guy and I were spending so much time together that he asked me to move in with him and I did. His mom didn't care and my foster grandmother was ready for me to go because I had been spending nights over there with him anyway and she wasn't having it. She warned me not to do it, but of course, I didn't listen. My flesh was ruling and I liked it. When I moved in with this man, the tide changed. This is when I discovered that my man was on drugs. He was a crackhead. WHAT??? I had been duped by a crackhead. It took a minute for me to get over the initial shock, but my man had "assured" me that he was doing crack recreationally. He wasn't hooked, he told me. He could control his drug use, he told me.

Do I have to tell y'all that he lied? After the revelation of his drug use, I decided to stay with him. I didn't know anything about crack and its effects on the user. I had no idea that crackheads stole from their loved ones and anybody else to get high. I didn't know about the paranoid episodes that would ensue. I had no idea that crackheads slept in crack houses and that if they didn't have the money to get high, that they slept with whomever was in the crack house to be able to get some crack.

Now, the Bishop and Pastor had dealt with this young man prior to me meeting him. When they realized I was in a serious relationship with him, they told me that he was a drug user. *Fine time to tell me after I had moved in.* They only disclosed this information to me because I was working for them and as the Administrative Assistant, I collected money (large sums) and they did not want my man to force me into stealing money from them to support his drug habit. I was offended to think that they did not trust me; that they thought I would give in to the demands of a crackhead. Well, they were right. I did take money one time to give to him and I felt like the lowest person on the face of the earth. A few days later, I was terminated, and rightly so. I was still a member of the church, but by now, everybody knew what I had done and nobody wanted to be bothered with me.

So, because of that, instead of me getting away from my man, he became my world. If the church didn't want to be bothered with me, then it would be me and him against the world. So I began smoking again. I would miss church a lot. I even began drinking. I was living the life now – *so I thought*.

As time went on, we got jobs at a company in Blue Bell, PA. We were making good money. I noticed my man started to act funny. He was always broke. I knew how much he made, because again, we worked at the same job. He would begin to demand MY check. I would wait for him to leave and then hide the money in another room, but he would find it and spend it on crack. Sometimes he would be gone for two or three days at a time. I tried to confide in his mom, but she seemed to condone his behavior. She would tell me that I had no business with him anyway, seeing as how I was a "Christian".

My man's crack habit had gotten so bad that I decided to leave him. I could not tolerate the stealing, paranoid episodes, and horrible mood swings. I hated the fact that he would get high and miss days from work. He would neglect his oral hygiene but would still expect to have sex. I had had enough.

Finally, I decided to move. When I packed my bags, he begged me to stay. He promised that he would stop using and that he would even go to church with me. I believed him. He seemed so sincere. So, for a minute, he stopped using but his mom had tired of us living there. So we moved out and lived around the corner from the church to live with his grandfather. Let me tell you how dumb I got. When I would go to church, I would hang around the church until everybody left because I didn't want anybody to know that we were living around the corner. Although they knew I was fornicating, I didn't want them all up in my business. But one day, the Bishop pulled me to the side and let me know that he knew we were shacking up and were living around the corner. He advised me to give up the relationship or get married because he didn't want me to bring shame on the church. He knew this guy was a drug user but those were the choices he gave me. I told my man what the Bishop had said and we decided to get married. Screech… Pump your breaks. It gets worse.

So, I informed the Bishop that me and my man were going to get married. The Pastor was not having it. She warned me not to get married to him. She told me that this marriage was not of GOD. She told me that if I married him I would go through hell. She didn't even go to the wedding (but I digress).

So, as the marriage time got closer, my man got cold feet. I tried to convince him that everything was going to be okay. I tried to persuade him to stop using the crack, but the more I nagged him, the more he did. I thought I could sex the desire for crack out of him, but it didn't work. I thought I could PRAY the desire to use crack out of him, but I was living in sin myself. I thought I could persuade him that if we got married that things would be better. I should have let his feet stay cold and ran for my life but I had wrapped my life, and my identity up in him. I was now CO-DEPENDENT. I thrived off of the misery that our lives had become. And yes, although I was miserable, I was too afraid to leave the relationship. I was too needy and too weak to leave him. So we continued on with the relationship and got married by the Bishop. The Pastor went out of town, on purpose, because she did not agree with her husband joining two nuts together in HOLY MATRIMONY.

On the night before the wedding, my man disappeared. I thought, he is really taking this cold feet thing too far. I didn't know where he was. I was afraid that he wouldn't show up for the wedding. I paced and paced. I called every number I had, looking for him. When I finally got in touch with him, I asked him if he was going to go through with this wedding. He was high – just coming down from it. He said that he didn't know, and then he said "YES, I'll be there" but something in his voice told me otherwise. So, fear kicked in and about every 20 minutes I would call him to see if he was still coming. After all, I was ready to get married although I knew deep within that I was marrying the WRONG MAN. I knew deep inside that this was NOT GOD'S will for me.

I knew deep inside that once I said "I DO," it was going to be hell to pay but because I was needy and co-dependent, and because I didn't want to continue to live in sin, I pushed away all of the warning signs and the advice of the Pastor and married this guy anyway. When I saw him come to the church, I was relieved because I didn't want to be the jilted woman at the altar.

We didn't have a honeymoon. We just went around the corner, made love, and then he went out and got high. I felt lower than low. I mean, we had just gotten married and now he is right back out there getting high. *GOD, WHAT HAVE I DONE?* Needless to say, things took a turn for the worse. After about a year of him constantly getting high, I got up enough courage to leave him. When he realized I was serious, he decided to go to rehab. This was the first of three trips to a rehab facility. Each time he'd go he would promise to change his ways. He would promise that when he came out of rehab, he would make it up to me. He swore that he would never use crack again. He knew just how to manipulate me and play on my emotions. Each time he came out, he'd be good for about a week and then he'd slowly go back to the crack. I wasn't his wife, the CRACK WAS.

After the last time of him going back to the crack, I snapped. I told him to give me some crack. I told him that if crack was all that then I need to start using it. He was shocked. He could not believe that I would tell him something like. But to my surprise, he refused to give me crack and begged me not to use. That made me feel good for a brief moment, but he had decided that he was done with rehabs and that he wasn't ready to stop using crack. *At that moment, I made up my mind to leave him for good. I made up my mind that no matter how many times he went to rehab again, this marriage was over. I packed my things, picked up the phone and called a friend. They picked me up and I never looked back.* I stayed with my friends for a while but I was in a bad way. I was depressed. Had lost so much weight that people began to think I had succumbed to crack. I was hopeless but where sin did abound, grace abounded much more. I pursued a divorce and it became final in 1998.

So I share this story with you to let you know that when GOD sends the warning, when HE shows you the signs that say danger, do not enter this relationship; when your pastor, bishop or somebody comes to you repeatedly and warns you not to marry this person; when you see messages on TV or billboards that make you think twice about marrying that person, **Please listen. Please pray. Please seek God with your whole heart, soul and body and run for your life. Obedience is better than sacrifice. Don't sell your birthright**…It's not worth it.

During this experience, GOD was telling me to look to HIM for the love I was so desperately seeking. GOD was clearly showing me that I was not ready for this or any relationship. I needed to turn my attention to GOD: what He wanted; How HE wanted to be the man in my life. GOD showed me that I needed healing in my soul. Being a foster child and going from home to home, I experienced rejection and abuse. I needed to be healed from the hate, anger, resentment, rejection and abuse. I wasn't fit for a relationship or marriage.

Fear of being alone is what kept me in the relationship so long. I needed to trust GOD and not fear the unknown. I needed to grow in OBEDIENCE TO GOD and not my feelings. I should have listened to THAT INNER VOICE OF WARNING FROM THE HOLY SPIRIT and I should have listened to my Bishop and

Pastor and NOT MARRIED him. From the beginning of the relationship God spoke to me, but I didn't understand at the time what I realize today- I DON'T NEED A MAN to be me. I am who GOD created me to be.

God had to even show me what was going on with the leadership at my old church. However, I wasn't seeking Him first- I was seeking their approval. I know in my heart that leadership did NOT handle that situation correctly. I never asked the Lord how HE felt about it but if someone knows that someone should not marry a particular person but does so anyway, hmmm. Honestly, he (the bishop) was trying to get me out of living in fornication but he should have listened to GOD and not his emotions.

My spiritual walk today is much different. I am learning who I am in Christ JESUS. I have learned to seek GOD and not listen to man (although I still fall short sometimes). I am learning that to really love GOD is to obey HIM in ALL THINGS – no matter how they look to man. Relationship wise, I am currently re-married and I just celebrated 12 years. We are both healing from some things from our pasts and currently believing GOD for manifestation of physical healing. *By HIS stripes ye WERE healed*...Isaiah 53

My Prayer

Heavenly Father, I come to You in the name of JESUS to thank You for delivering me from the bonds of sin. Heavenly Father, I thank You for allowing me to go through this situation and to be able to use it to help somebody else who may find themselves in a similar situation.

Heavenly Father, I lift up the person or people who are contemplating marrying the wrong person and I ask You, in the name of JESUS to speak to them by Your Holy Spirit and let them know that this is not YOUR will.

Heavenly Father, I come against the spirit of pride, rebellion/witchcraft, disobedience, fear of loneliness, co-dependency, every mind-binding spirit, spiritual blindness, spiritual deafness, fornication, deceiving spirits, spiritual wickedness in high places, rulers of darkness of this world, wicked imaginations, every high thing that exalts itself against the knowledge of GOD; the spirit of error and false teaching; and the lust of the eyes, the lust of the spirit, and the pride of life spirits, and I command you come out in the name of JESUS!!! Loose GOD'S PEOPLE and let them go, in the name of JESUS, AMEN.

~Evangelist Theresa Scott

Dear Lord, I Think I Married The Wrong Person

Reverend Dawn Williams

With the spirit of a watchwoman, Reverend Dawn Michelle Williams is an ordained Minister of the Gospel. She is a Teacher, Preacher and Kingdom Intercessor. She is the wife of Mr. Robert L. Williams and the proud mother of two beautiful daughters, Brittany and Adara. Two of the greatest influences in her life are her father Pastor Clinton Brown, Sr. and her mother Maggie Brenda Whittaker.

Rev. Dawn was educated in the Chesapeake Public School System where she received an Advanced Academic Diploma in 1988. After graduating from Deep Creek High School she attended Old Dominion University where she obtained her B.S. in Interdisciplinary Studies and her M.S. in Elementary Education. For the past twelve years, she has dedicated her life to educating young people. She has been honored twice for her hard work and dedication by being named as Campostella Elementary's 2002 Teacher of the Year and Granby Elementary's 2007 Teacher of the Year.

Rev. Dawn is a member *Grace Fellowship Worship Center* where the Founder and Pastor is none other than Rev. Dr. James E. Jones, Jr. and Elder Cheryl B. Jones. She currently serves as the Pastor of Women's Ministry.

Rev. Dawn was licensed to preach the Gospel on April 10, 2005 at *First Baptist Church Bolling Brook* under the leadership of her father Pastor Clinton Brown, Sr. She served there faithfully as the Youth Pastor for four years. During her tenure at "The Brook" she established a Youth Bible Study Group, Youth Open Mic Night, and the Big Things Poppin, Foolish Things Stoppin Summer Workshop.

Rev. Dawn is also the founder of *From Dusk-2-Dawn Women's* Ministry. Through the birthing of this ministry in 2007, God truly gave her beauty for her ashes. As the founder and leader of this ministry God has called her to equip and empower women emotionally, physically, financially, and spiritually. To that end, From *Dusk-2-Dawn Women's* Ministry strives to provide women with a support network of hope, healing and encouragement.

Rev. Dawn stands on the scripture 1 Corinthians 9:16 *"For if I preach the gospel I have nothing to boast of for necessity is laid upon me; yes woe is me if I do not preach the gospel!"*

For booking information contact :

Call: FromDusk2Dawn Ministries (757) 401-3136

        or

Email: Dusk2Dawn07@aol.com

Dear Lord, I Think I Married The Wrong Person

Two Halves, Don't Make A Whole

On November 4, 1995 I had no idea how a casual meeting at Brown's Convenience store would shape the next ten years of my life. At this particular time in my life I had no interest in meeting anyone. I was focused on one goal; completing my Master's in Education so that I could create a better life for me and my seven year old daughter. Brown's Convenience store was our family business and I begged my uncle to give me a job on the weekends while I was completing my student teaching experience. His convenience store was located right outside of Gate 4 of the Norfolk Naval Base so he gave me one condition when he hired me. He said under no circumstances are you to get involved with any navy guy that comes in this store. I agreed wholeheartedly because that was definitely not a part of my plan.

Plan interrupted…One night while I was working this navy guy walks in and introduces himself to me; he asked me my name and before I could say anything the young lady who was working with me said, "This is Mr. Brown's niece." Apparently, he had been a frequent customer in Brown's Convenience Store and everyone knew that anyone that was related to Mr. Brown was off limits. However, that didn't stop this young man from trying to get his "flirt on."

Dear Lord, I Think I Married The Wrong Person

When he saw me he immediately went into his "mack daddy" role. He kept going on and on about how pretty I was. He decided that he was going to go home and get his older brother. His exact words were, "I know my brother is going to love you!" He proceeded to leave the store and a few minutes later he came back with his brother. They both continued to flirt with me and left their number for me to call. He said, "You can call him or me, either way you won't lose" *I had no idea, but that was the first lie of many - I lost a lot.* They left and I went back to work without giving either one of them any further thought.

That lasted for about 20 minutes, the phone rang and "the little brother" was back at it again. I told him I was busy so he asked if I would give him a call when I got off work. I agreed, but I really had no intention of calling. However, the young lady that I was working with *who was not saved and had no business giving me advice* proceeded to convince me that I should give one of them a call.

The little brother was really not my type, back then I was interested in the light skinned curly haired brothers *Oh, I wish I knew then what I know now. My type would have had nothing to do with looks and everything to do with character.* When I got home I must admit the older brother was on my mind. It was something about him. As luck or un-luck would have I decided to call that evening and the big brother answered the phone. We spent the whole night talking on the phone getting to know one another better. He was one year younger than I, just recently medically discharged from the Navy, and a divorced father of two *so I thought* .

Dear Lord, I Think I Married The Wrong Person

The relationship took off like rockets. We began to see each other almost every day. He lived down the street from Brown's Convenience store so every time I went to work he was right there. About three months into the relationship I found out that I was pregnant. I was so disappointed that I allowed my flesh to get me off track yet again. We made plans to move in together and that's when his web of deception began to unravel.

The man that I had been involved with and was now carrying his child had given me an alias. His name was not the name that I had been calling him for the last three months, he was not legally divorced and he was not the father of two children, but three children. His oldest son was by his first wife, (yes, I said first wife) and he had two children by his current wife.

I should have ran for my life and never looked back. I contemplated cutting my losses, but I was pregnant and I already had one child out of wedlock and I didn't want to repeat the same history. I will never forget the day I found out at my Family Reunion. It was so humiliating. One of my cousins had been in the Navy at the same time he was in the Navy and she was on the same ship with him and his wife. It was a lot of whispering going on at the Family Reunion behind my back. Then the whisper finally came to me, "Dawn is pregnant by a married man!" My heart shattered into a million and one pieces. I confronted him and of course he lied. He came up with some story about his ex-wife never turning in the divorce papers and he didn't know anything about it. He promised me that he would get a divorce right away and we would get married as soon as his divorce was final. Well that didn't happen until two years later.

Dear Lord, I Think I Married The Wrong Person

After two years of living on an emotional roller coaster. I decided that I just couldn't take living in sin any longer. I had started going back to church on a regular basis and I was being convicted each and every time I set foot in the sanctuary. I finally had the courage to tell him that we were going to have to get married or go our separate ways. Separate ways should have been my choice, because this man was abusive to me verbally and physically. I should have left him the time he beat me up so bad that I couldn't go to work for a week. I should have left him the time he fought me and my brother and we both ended up with stitches. I should have left him the time he flattened all my tires and busted the windows out of my car. I should have left him when I found out that he was addicted to telling lies. **I SHOULD HAVE LEFT, I SHOULD HAVE LEFT, I SHOULD HAVE LEFT!**

I was under the misconception that leaving would have been a defeat and I did not want to be defeated. I did not want to have two kids and not be married to either one of their fathers.

I wanted to be married so bad that it clouded every ounce of my discernment and judgment. I was about to make the worst decision of my life and I used the word of God to justify it. "The word says it's better to marry than to burn!" It was my hope that the Lord would honor me trying to do the right thing. He agreed that we would get married as soon as he could buy a ring. About a month later we went to the justice of the peace and got married. I didn't tell anyone, because I knew my family and friends would think I was crazy. For the most part everyone that was close to me wanted me out of this relationship.

Dear Lord, I Think I Married The Wrong Person

Before I met him I was an outgoing person who loved to spend time with my friends and family. They watched me turn into a person that they could barely recognize. I rarely spent any time with my family or my friends. He was so insecure that he alienated me from everyone. He always thought I was up to something. He was the big liar, but yet he always accused me of lying. In the back on my mind I knew that I was doing the wrong thing, but I didn't listen to that "still small voice."

The first year of the marriage was actually pretty good, we had been living together for two years so nothing really changed, except that we both made an extra effort to try and please one another now that we were married. After the first year he became a little distant. He said that he was tired of the routine. Our life had become boring. Little did I know that he had found excitement elsewhere.

I don't remember how, but I found out about this girl that he was talking to. I gave her a call and she assured me that they were just friends. She thought I knew about her. He told her that we were having problems and he needed someone to talk to. I had put up with so much deception in this relationship that something in me just cracked. I didn't feel the same way about him from that day forward. We tried to make it work, but I just didn't trust him. I finally mustered up the courage to ask him to leave and he agreed.

It was a difficult decision but I decided to move to Atlanta with my mother and start a new life for myself. This new life was absent of the God who had just brought me out. I totally forgot about God and was living in a backslidden state of mind. I was like a bird that had just been let out of the cage. I wanted to spread my wings and that is exactly what I did. I was partying like it was 1999. "But God had another plan!!!" On Sunday, November 24, 2002, my 32nd birthday at New Birth Missionary Baptist Church in Lithonia, Georgia at the 10:30am service I gave my life back to God "for real" and I knew there was no turning back.

I can remember it now just like it was yesterday. The text was Numbers 13 and the title of the sermon was *"You Make the Choice: Stay in Egypt or Go to the Promise Land."* I made the choice that day to go to the Promise Land I have never looked back. When I came to Atlanta I was like "Humpty Dumpty broken into a million pieces." But on November 24, 2002 the King of Kings put the pieces back together again. I rededicated my life to the Lord that day. It was different than any other time I had come to the Lord before. I knew that my life would never be the same again. I started attending church every Sunday. I attended 5am prayer. I took a spiritual gifts class. I was like a sponge soaking up all the word I could. I began to have dreams and visions of myself preaching the word of God. My life was changed and it was good.

I was in total shock when I heard the spirit of the Lord clearly say, "It's time to go back home." Why would God want to send me back to the place of brokenness? I had become whole again. One Sunday it became so clear. The word from the Lord was it's time to re-dig your father's well. I knew that word was for me and that the Lord was sending me back to Virginia to work in my father's church. I had learned so much about ministry that it was time for me to put it to use. So that summer I made the big move back to VA. I knew the Lord was on my side because I obtained a teaching position at the exact school that I told the Lord I wanted to teach in 11 years prior. This was the school that I had successfully completed my student teaching experience, but I was afraid to apply for the job because I was pregnant and not married. When I began considering the move I said to the Lord that was the place I wanted to teach…Full circle!

Everything fell into place upon my return. I re-joined my father's church and I immediately became involved with the youth ministry. I accepted my calling and on April 10, 2005 at First Baptist Church Bolling Brook I preached my initial sermon (with my ex-husband in the congregation cheering me on) The title was, *"Are You Ready to Crossover?"* The evidence that I was called was affirmed by a life coming to Christ that day. I am still amazed that He chose me, and each time that I stand to teach/preach His word and I see lives being transformed I am humbled that He took a messed up girl like me who ran away from Him as hard as I could to speak to His people. That's why I stand on the scripture I Corinthians 9:16 *" For if I preach the gospel I have nothing to boast of for necessity is laid upon me; yes woe is me if I do not preach the gospel!*

All of a sudden the Youth Pastor at the church announced that he was leaving so I assumed my natural position as the leader of the youth ministry. Things were going so well, too good in fact. The enemy was mad as hell and he didn't want to let me fulfill the purpose of God in my life. Too many lives were being transformed and saved.

Dear Lord, I Think I Married The Wrong Person

My ex-husband began to pursue me with a fervor I had never witness in him before. Everything that I ever wanted him to say or do- he said and did. He even came to my Dad's church and got baptized. He was Catholic, so I thought this must be God. Little did I know he was wooing me right back into darkness. The same man who delivered divorce papers to me on Mother's Day two years earlier was taking me to a house that he wanted to buy for me on Mother's Day two years later.

I finally decided to give our marriage another try. This time we got married in Church in the presence of God and a few family members and friends. What a marvelous thing the Lord was doing? *Not!* This time it only took two weeks before I realized that this was not God restoring what the enemy had stolen. This was a trick of the enemy to distract me from my purpose. I had just made the second worse mistake of my life.

The second time around there was no physical abuse just verbal abuse. I think he knew that I would not accept being physically abused so his abuse became more subtle. He began to attack my character and my commitment to God. He would do things to push my buttons and then when I would react. He would say, "I thought you were saved." I felt so defeated which is exactly where the enemy wanted me to be.

The same man who had cheered me on when I preached my initial sermon had now come to the conclusion that he didn't like being married to a preacher. He didn't like people looking up to me and calling me for spiritual guidance. He didn't want to share me with the church.

Dear Lord, I Think I Married The Wrong Person

Dear Lord, what have I done? I thought this was you giving me another chance at the family that I have always wanted. How did I get back to this place of bondage and despair? How God? Why did you let me do this? If you get me out of this Lord I promise I will run and never look back. I remember listening to a message by Juanita Bynum. She declared that if her marriage didn't work it was going to go on record that she left with clean hands and I wanted that to be my testimony too so I went into Spiritual Warfare mode.

I bought the book, *The Power of a Praying Wife.* I began to diligently pray for my husband. The more I prayed the worse things got. Every time I had to preach he would start an argument with me the night before. I would get up in the pulpit after being called everything but a child of God, and Preach the word like nothing was wrong. I remained faithful. Through it all I continued to treat him better than he treated me. I continued to cry out to the Lord to deliver him or deliver me.

This is the part where I have to make an indictment on "church folk." They always want to say "stay." If the unbelieving spouse wants to stay in the marriage then you have to stay. No matter how miserable you are or how much abuse you have to take. I want to go on record and say that is a lie from the pit of hell. I do not believe it is God's desire for his children to stay in unhealthy, unproductive, and ungodly marriages. Yes, the word does say what God has joined together let no man put asunder. But this mess right here was not ordained by God. It was all me.

Thank God that He will always make a way of escape for you. Thank God that everything that's done in the dark will eventually come to the light. My husband began having another affair just like he had done when we were married the first time. Again, I decided to make contact with the other woman and my suspicions were confirmed. Within minutes of me calling her he came home yelling and screaming and very belligerent. I didn't say a word. He grabbed some things and left. That night I moved out of our bedroom and moved into the guest room upstairs. The next few months were spent on my face seeking God like never before. I wanted to hear clear instructions from the Lord.

From September to November we slept in separate bedrooms. He came and went as he pleased. He would stay out all night and then come home the next morning singing love songs. I thought I was going to lose my mind. *But God!* One day he came home with a separation agreement that he want me to sign. It entitled me to absolutely nothing. He wanted me to leave the house by December 31st with nothing but the clothes on my back. I will never forget the day I heard clear instructions from the Lord. I was on my face praying in the spirit. The Lord told me to sign the separation agreement.

I had no idea where I was going to live or how this decision would affect my life and the life of my children, but I trusted God. I received confirmation that I was making the right decision when I found out that my Godmother's mother had a room for rent that had been empty since August. Her mother had let the room go un-rented for 4 months because the spirit of the Lord told her that I was going to need it. Wow God! Wow!

Dear Lord, I Think I Married The Wrong Person

    It was the most humbling experience to have to leave the first home that I had ever purchased as an adult. A home that I help decorate, picked out the carpets, painted the walls, and hung family photos. A home that my daughter loved. When she first saw the backyard with that in ground pool I thought she was going to lose her mind. The place that I had testified about, this was the Lord's doing to bring my family back together, what I was going to say now? I didn't have to say anything. God took care of it all. I didn't wait until December 31st to leave that house. I left on December 1st, because I wanted to end and start my New Year off right. I traveled back to Atlanta over the Holidays and received further confirmation that *He that had begun a good work in me was going to complete it!*

    Granted, there were consequences to my disobedience. The most difficult part of this experience was taking my daughters back into an unhealthy environment. In fact my oldest daughter ended up leaving me and going to live with her father for about 6 months into the second marriage. She hated the way my ex-husband talked to me. The day she left it was like my heart was being ripped out of my chest. She looked me right in my face and said "Momma, why do you let him talk to you like that?" "Don't you know that you deserve better?" I did know, but I wasn't ready to make the difficult choices that I needed to make at that point to change my circumstances. Thank God that both of my daughters witnessed God deliver me from this unhealthy, ungodly, unproductive union not once, but twice. They have seen God give me beauty for my ashes through the birthing of *FromDusk2Dawn Women's Ministry*.

Dear Lord, I Think I Married The Wrong Person

As the founder and leader of this ministry God has allowed me to use my trials and tribulations to equip and empower women emotionally, physically, financially, and spiritually. From Dusk-2-Dawn Women's Ministry was birthed during one of the darkest seasons of my life which is why we strive to provide women with a support network of hope, healing and encouragement.

God truly spared me from worse circumstances. I truly believe that God hardened my ex-husband's heart towards me to give me enough time to make an "intelligent decision." We had been in and out and back and forth of this love-hate relationship for 10 years. Even my family thought that he was going to try and get me back just like he had done many times before, but thanks be to God he didn't. When I left that house in December of 2005 I never looked back and he never tried to get me back. It was finally over, because God said it was over. From 1995 to 2005 it was a never ending emotional roller coaster, 3 years of marriage 7 years of turbulence. 10 years... 10 is the number of completion. That chapter of my life was complete and it was time for me to begin a new chapter.

The Lord revealed "me to me" during this time. I wanted my life to be defined by being the perfect wife and perfect mother. I wanted the white picket fence. I had the Barbie syndrome. Originally, it was my insecurity that was the root cause of all this chaos. Not realizing that just being who God called me to be was enough. I felt like I had to be married to one of my children's fathers in order to complete the story. But whose story was that?

Dear Lord, I Think I Married The Wrong Person

That's the American Dream, that's the story that we are fed as a little girl into adulthood and I bought it hook line and sinker.

My family always said to me even from a young age that I was probably going to be the first to get married. Even at a young age I loved children. I was always the teenager walking around with a baby on my hip. I wanted to do it the right way. I wanted to get married and then have children but I did it backwards. So I spent all my energy focused on trying to right that wrong- when all I had to do was accept God's forgiveness and His Grace and move on. I tried to right a wrong with another wrong. I thought that I was whole and complete with Christ, but as I said earlier there were some places in me that were not completely healed and that opened the door for my ex-husband to come back in.

I learned to rely on the Holy Spirit. I learned how to spend time in prayer travailing before the Lord. I learned that success is not measured by what kind of car you drive or what kind of house you live in. More importantly I learned that, *All things work together for the good of them who loved the Lord and are called according to His purpose.*

I learned that healing and deliverance doesn't always happen overnight and you have to allow time for God to do a work in you. I learned to lean not to my own understanding, but in all my ways acknowledge Him so that He could direct my path. I learned that greater is He that is in me than he that is in the world. I learned that weeping may endure for a night, but Joy comes in the morning. I learned that God will allow you to do whatever it is you want to do even if He knows it's not the best thing for you. He will not usurp our free will. He will speak in a still small voice and it's up to us to listen and obey.

If I could turn back the hands of time I wouldn't change a thing. My power was created by my pain. My ability to hear from God was created in my despair. My prayer life was fine-tuned and developed during the most hellacious stage of my life. He is my strength, and my peace. I learned the true meaning of His Grace being sufficient. I trust Him with my whole heart and I have committed my ways to Him. Every gift and anointing that He has bestowed upon me I vow to use it for His glory and to advance the Kingdom of God.

After my obedience, God honored my heart's desire- to be married, and to have a complete family, but this time I married the man God had for me, and who could truly appreciate me. On July 4, 2011 I got married to a wonderful man who celebrates the call on my life. He encourages me in ministry. He builds me up instead of tearing me down. He recognizes who I am in God and he knows that he found his "good thing!"

"Behold, I will do a new thing; now it shall spring forth; shall ye not know it? I will even make a way in the wilderness, and rivers in the desert."

God is truly doing a new thing in my life. It took me 40 years to get to the place where I truly understood my value. I was at a place in my life where I was "Single and Satisfied." Although, I didn't write the book. I was living the sentiment. As an unmarried woman I was caring for the things of the Lord. While I had anticipation that my Boaz was coming, I was not out looking for him. My God ordained husband found me. He actually sought me out. Our paths originally crossed when I was 16 and he was 24. I was only in his company one time, but he never forgot about me.

On December 28, 2009 (24 years later) he made contact with my sister on Facebook and asked her about me. She never replied to his request so he went through the pictures on her page and found one that I was tagged in. (Single Ladies…He was looking for me, he found me!) He sent me a friend request and 14 months later we were married. When people ask how he knew I was the one for him his famous reply is, "It don't take all day to recognize sunshine." This man celebrates me, he encourages me, and he builds me up. He wants to see my ministry successful. Simply put, "He lets me be me." I have never experienced that in my life. Everyone I have ever dated in the past wanted to change me into "Their Dawn" but Robert L. Williams lets me be "The Dawn" that God created me to be and I am so excited about our future

Dear Lord,

I come to you on behalf of every woman that has just come to the realization that they married the wrong man. First and foremost God I ask that you deliver them from man's opinion. For we know that man looks on the outward appearance, but you are concerned with the heart. Lord, heal their broken heart and bind up all their wounds. God just as you gave me clear instructions I ask that you speak directly to them. Give them an ear to hear what the spirit is saying concerning their marriage. Whether you deliver them in it or deliver them out of it. I pray that you give them the courage to accept what you are saying. I know that you can cause all things to work together for the God of them who love you and are called according to your purpose. What you did for me, Father, do it for them. Let them know that you are not a respecter of persons and that you are able to do exceedingly, abundantly above all they can either ask or think. Do it God! Do it In Jesus Name, Amen!

This time around I got "Better" not "Bitter!" I don't blame my ex-husband for our marriage not working. I think we both were two halves trying to make a whole. That formula may work when building fractions, but not when you are trying to build a marriage.

~Reverend Dawn Williams

Bobbie Clark – Alexander

is a multifaceted energetic woman grounded in her Christian faith as a speaker & lecturer, counselor, author, educator, business consultant, prophetic end-time coach and marketplace vessel appointed and anointed of God for the 21st Century. Impacting lives of divorced single moms, families, businesses, churches, marketplace, and political arenas through ResourceWoman.com LLC, a new equipping agency being set in place to meet all the points of interest and endowments Bobbie possesses, through teaching workshops, personal and group counseling, business consulting, and economic empowerment.

In her resiliency to keep bouncing back after several life setbacks and a failed marriage, this woman still packed punches through secular and Christian posts held such as a top sheet accountant with IBM in Southbury, CT; accountant with the City of New Orleans; standardize test scorer for various school districts throughout the U.S. with Pearson Education Services, Atlanta, GA; Business Consultant in New Orleans, LA and Atlanta, GA to companies and entrepreneurs; held various Christian leadership and teaching roles in her home mega ministry church of 15 years in New Orleans, LA before relocating to Atlanta in 2003.

Bobbie has earned numerous degrees, which give her a competitive edge on her peers and every area she services making her calling sure: Master of Arts in Education, specialization in curriculum design and post-secondary student counseling; Master of Arts in Human Service Counseling (HSC); 24 hours currently completed of MBA in Global Entrepreneurship from Regent University, Virginia Beach, VA; Bachelor of Science in Accounting, minor in Business Administration from Xavier University of Louisiana.

Bobbie and her two children currently reside in Atlanta, GA.

Contact Info:

Bobbie Clark-Alexander, M.Ed., MA-HSC, BS
P.O. Box 83436
Conyers, GA 30013

Website: www.ResourceWoman.com
Facebook "Like" Fan Page Bobbie Clark-Alexander, Author
Follow on Twitter @bclarkalexander
Email: bclarkalexander@yahoo.com

Don't Get Got! Things are Not Always the Way They Appear.

I was married for 16 years to a man who had many secrets. However, I did not learn of the secrets or was equipped to identify them until I found myself in unthinkable emotional pain during the last five years of my marriage, each year harder to deal with then the last. I thought that I knew the man I married; to only find out I knew only what he showed me and not who he really was. I married a hard worker, provider, law abiding, and loving man who seemed more than reasonable by the church and world standard during this particular generation.

My husband was born into and practiced Catholicism and I traditional Baptist, neither one of us were on fire for God at the time we married. I ended up leaving the Baptist church when I met my husband because I became discouraged by the endless scandals of monies stolen from the church treasury, and the plethora of sexual and adulterous indiscretions, to find the same events in the Catholic Church under a different guise and not as blatant until exposed.

I was longing for a love to fill a big hole inside of me, something apparently missed during childhood-my father was missing in action (MIA) and my husband to be seemed to fill the void. Today, I realize that Jesus was knocking on the door of my heart for all of me and no longer just part of me. At the time, I could not accept or receive counsel from a praying grandmother that told me I should date and marry a minister. Most of what I saw and heard about the male clergy in the circles fellowshipped in was distasteful events that I did not want any parts of. So, subconsciously I was drawn towards the lies and trickery of the enemy for what appeared to be good and right in a man, but not whole and holy, what God wanted for me.

I married my husband because I received and experienced a love of a male never experienced in my life prior to the age of 18. When I met my husband, he wowed me off of my feet. Wined and dined me, always paying for the meals, nightclub cover charges, and movies. On my birthday and Christmas I received beautiful pieces of jewelry from him and was simply treated like the queen I was. I lacked the prerequisites of being a princess through the love of a father, being told by him how beautiful I was and being adorned with gifts and all my hearts' desire before I became a queen. I eventually began to realize after the divorce that I needed that authentication and validation from a father figure. My mother and grandmother always told me how beautiful I was, and furnished me with beautiful things my entire childhood. But it felt a whole lot different coming from a man who wanted to give me the world and treated me like the royal priesthood I already was a part of in the Kingdom of God, but did not know it.

I did not understand that a good hard working man who treated me well was not enough. The teachings from the local churches I attended did not include 2 Corinthians 6:14 about being unequally yoked with unbelievers and what that consisted of, or being a part of a royal priesthood and chosen generation, a holy nation in I Peter 2:9.

In spite of spiritual error during my childhood rearing, the four books of the Gospel were hidden down in my heart, grounding me foundationally to be the sold out for Jesus individual I am today. Many summers of vacation bible school, Christmas and Easter plays, reciting scripture, actually placed me miles ahead of my husband spiritually. Though very traditional and void of the Holy Spirit for the most part, I took my spiritual practices and beliefs for granted and saw them of little value. I believed I was not any better than my husband, even though he was void of God's Word in his life. In essence, I did not know who I was. I did not know that I was to be set apart and only consider a marriage partner who had a *real* relationship with God through His Word and life giving, mind transforming Holy Spirit.

Marriage and family were a childhood envy of mine because I never experienced what it felt like to have both parents in the home. My father left my mother when I was three ½ years old, and I have little to no memory of his presence in our home or visitations after that time. Once on my way to church utilizing public transit, my father flirted with me from approximately 50 feet distance, not knowing it was his 16-year old daughter he hadn't seen in several years. I cannot remember anything else from that incident because that was something I wanted to forget forever.

I met my husband at the first company I worked for right out of high school. I participated in the Cooperative Office Education (COE) program offered through the public school system where high school students participated in a pre-professional clerical training program that prepared us over a three year period to land a corporate position by senior year of high school. Mostly major corporations and governmental agencies in the city partnered with the program causing wonderful opportunities for me and so many others to obtain great positions.

Apparently my husband to-be watched me as I stepped off the public transit reporting to work each day around noon after attending morning classes. I had to pass in front of his building to get to my office, though it was the same company. He was 4 years older than me, definitely with more experience with females.

Literally, it was the old school wooing that got my attention. At first I didn't pay him much attention. However, the compliments daily were ones I had not heard from my high school peers, nor my high school sweetheart that I had just broke up with who eventually also landed a job at the same company. *Talking about a three ring circus that I was definitely not equipped to handle.* Between the two men beckoning for my attention, there was literally no competition between them and the more experienced silver tongue older guy won out.

I dated my ex-husband for 3 years before he proposed marriage to me. During this time, we broke up a few times because the same ex-girlfriend would resurface at least once a year. It appeared that she realized she loved and wanted him because he was with me. In retrospect, I now know I was the rebound and should have broken things off with him for good once I gained knowledge of this information. But I was too young to understand the repercussions of such a situation. Also, believing the lies he told me that things were finished. He said that ex-girlfriend needed someone to talk to because her mother had died when she was a young child. I bought into the lies and confusion because he always had a way to make up with me by taking me nice places and bringing roses from his grandmother's garden. No man had ever treated me as such. So it appeared sincere, plus it felt good to the emotional holes in my life from the absent father. The attention was like a longing from the well of my soul. My father never gave me a single rose, not even from someone's yard.

    The first 10 years of my marriage were wonderful. Our home was the hosting place for many family events and every major holiday celebration. By this time, I had found my way back home in the spiritual environment God needed me to be in. One Wednesday night I went to support a college friend give her first sermon in a full gospel Baptist church. The service was wonderful and one I had never experienced growing up in the traditional Baptist environment; their teachings seem to include all the scriptures, not only the ones comfortable to the flesh. A couple months later on Christmas Day, I walked the middle isle of this church and said "Happy Birthday Jesus"! I knew almost instantly, the decision I had just made came with rewards and responsibility. This was also the day that marked the beginning of the end of my marriage unknowingly to both of us.

Dear Lord, I Think I Married The Wrong Person

I grew by leaps and bounds spiritually, realizing that I wasn't just saved, but born again, being filled with the Holy Spirit of God. I was no longer a fence walker in my faith, but sold out and on fire for Jesus. Even the nuns in the Catholic Church had seen there was something different about me during my 10 year practicing tenure and appointed me as the only lay leader of a bible study group. Looking back in retrospect that was an identification of who I was in God, but did not have a clue.

After a couple years, my husband joined the full gospel church to possibly be on one accord, as we always seemed to function in our home and marriage. However, there was never an apparent change in his desire or willingness to know or study the Word of God and learn the life of Christ. I saw this, but did not have a clue of the secret it would expose.

My elevation spiritually in God was rapid. I spent a year studying the bible, being trained directly by the Holy Spirit to pray and intercede on many heavenly matters God wanted wrought in the earth. I did not have any idea what God was training me for. With a love for marriage and family, the teaching of the senior pastor, I was surprisingly able to keep a balance with my time at church and home. Within 3 years I was in prophetic training, intercessory leader in a 25k member ministry, teaching intercessory workshops at local churches, running a viable business consulting firm in my home office, and jumping airplanes speaking across the nation.

There was a high anointing inside of me to do some serious spiritual warfare. Identifying the enemy miles away and walking in the authority of Jesus, casting a demon out in almost a whisper was a way of life for me. As God continued to elevate me spiritually, it became painfully clear that I did not have the huge space in my husband's heart anymore. There was still much intimacy in the bedroom, but his mind seemed to be on the other side of town. The intimacy began to dwindle slowly but surely.

He stopped coming straight home from work after his 3-11pm shift. The male friends he hung out with never came to the house, but he always met them at a club, movie theatre, etc. I began to hurt deeply inside because of the void and attention I always received from my husband. During this period, I realized that things got a little off once I announced I was pregnant with our first child. It's as if my husband just wanted it to be us for the entire marriage. Repeatedly, I would ask him what was wrong and he continually lied saying nothing was wrong, but that we were both just changing and it would all work out and be alright. But things continually got worse.

My husband then began to tell me that he didn't marry a preacher; I would continually try to explain that we don't have a choice once we submit and surrender our lives to Christ. That whatever the call was on our lives, we as born again Christians pick up the mantle of whatever our call was and follow Jesus. He protested that I did have a choice, and that I wanted to do it. "Oh My God," I thought, *what in the world is this*?

A perverted spirit straight from hell is what it was! Merriman Webster defines perverted as (of a thing) having been corrupted or distorted from its original course, meaning, or state.

Dear Lord, I Think I Married The Wrong Person

Everything in our lives that was once okay or going well was now all wrong according to my husband. He began to make up every excuse in the world why he was behaving the way he was. So I stopped attending evening church service, conferences, and most other functions affiliated with the ministry to be home and show him that my marriage and family were important and that God is not in the business of destroying homes.

To no avail, I then realized that my husband refused the power, love, and invitation of Jesus Christ and did not want Him in our home, bed, and lives. The dark secret in him had deceived my husband and convinced him that I was the enemy, which in essence I was. The light of Jesus in me had become so bright; it became literally impossible for that spirit of perversion to hide. Not long after this epiphany and revelation, the pain and void, the loss and love from my husband, the months of no intimacy lead me to a 21 day fast where I literally bombarded heaven to deliver my husband and save my marriage.

During the fast, God showed me that He allowed me to marry the man that would do the least amount of damage to me. He showed me that I was insistent on marriage and nothing would have stopped me. I then apprehended in the spirit during this fast that the emotional pain and suffering I was experiencing could have been much worse. That by being married to my husband, I was protected from the many men hell had set to inundate my life and destroy me spiritually, physically, and drive me out of mind so that I could not fulfill the mandate and purposes of God in the earth.

Dear Lord, I Think I Married The Wrong Person

My life changing encounter with God during the fast was then penned in my first book, *21 Days to Deliverance: Do I Stay, Fray, or Leave?* where I give transparent dialogue of how the gut wrenching emotional pain showed me the truth and that my marriage was not ordained of God, but permitted and used to bring me to where I stand today.

I also found out that my husband had parts of his life that he never talked about. He had very few stories from childhood that I began to understand were too painful for him to remember. The differences in our child rearing decisions now began to make sense to me. I was raised and reared in a structured, traditional, and spiritual setting where church was a part of our Sundays and Jesus was on the menu every day of the week. I then knew I had not waited on God and married the wrong person. The yearning for love of an earthly father was the culprit. I did not allow Jesus to fill the void, but a man who had not been fashioned nor chosen for me, plus I was very premature in marrying anyone. I was literally reared to be the wife of a leader and man of great influence; a man who could carry and support me naturally and spiritually. The man I chose did the best that he knew how, but was not willing to be stretched and delivered in Jesus.

I now thank my ex-husband for covering and protecting me and our kids financially, and me from the wolves of hell for 16 years until I matured in the understanding and obedience to the things of God for my life. However, the price tag that I paid for not waiting on the perfect will of God for my life was the emotional abuse I suffered at the hands of my husband who really didn't see the damage he was doing to me because he was not equipped to be "MY" husband.

My focus should have been on obtaining my education to be best qualified for what my God, life, and destiny held. I remember so many days in the middle of discussions with my husband when I shared my emotional pain and what his actions were doing to me, he would look at me like I was a crazy person. It was if he was from another world. One day, he went as far as to say that, "If I thought someone didn't want or love me anymore, I wouldn't want them anymore either." I'm thinking, "What the hell is this?" He was not ever planning on leaving our home, but expected me to sit there and do whatever his heart desired.

The mind games were endless where I thought I would lose my mind. I had sleepless nights, high blood pressure, short tempered with our children, hospital emergency room visit because my heart was about to jump out of my chest, and the list goes on. I was living in a hell on earth right in my own home, and my husband came and left our home like nothing was wrong and life was wonderful.

The plan was to kill me mentally, spiritually, emotionally where I would no longer be fit for any man, God, a mother to my children or myself. Toxic is what it was! But one day I managed to calm down enough to hear so clearly in my God conscientiousness that what my husband wanted I did not possess and never would. Everything was my fault for his actions and behaviors. That was the day I realized my marriage was over. However, it's as if I didn't matter anymore, and God needed me to be a go between for Him and my husband. So I immediately phoned my husband at work and told him I really needed to speak with him that night after work and he concurred affirmatively!

Later that night in my home far away from our children's bedrooms I engaged in a very soft tone selfless conversation with my husband. I somehow knew that it wasn't about me anymore strangely enough. I began to see my husband through another set of eyes, which had to be God's. The love and concern in my voice, heart, and mind had to be heaven sent because I could have never in my own flesh operated as such after all I had suffered emotionally and mentally at the hands of my husband.

I remember talking and asking a dialogue of questions about his childhood, and did something happen to violate his personhood? That if he wanted to get some sound professional counseling that I would go through it with him and be patient, not that I had to be in any of the sessions with him, but as long as I knew he was getting the help needed. He sat there staring at me with his mouth shut so tight as if it had been cemented shut. I literally got on my knees in front of him beseeching and literally pleading, even begging him to say something, just talk to me.

After a few minutes of silence and me kneeling on the floor at his feet crying and praying, all of a sudden from my gut, I vomited out my insides and became so weak that I slid in the slimy colorless fluids that had come up out of me. I couldn't have imagined the sight of it all, but as my husband look down at me, I could see fear and confusion in his eyes, but nothing still came out of his mouth. He picked me up off the floor and carried me to our bedroom in placed me in the bed. All the life was out of me and too weak to speak or do anything for myself. As I lay there, a feeling of freedom, weightlessness, peace, and calm came over me that I had not felt in years.

That was it! My 16 year marriage had been annulled in the heavens and I was freed by God and not man or myself. It was not very long after that point that my husband and I were physically separated. God had me to ask my husband to forgive me of anything he felt I had done and wish him the very best. But most importantly, I let him know that Jesus loves him and that I wish he could someday find it in his heart to receive Jesus as Lord and Savior of and over his life.

My matriarchal grandmother died about 3 months before my wedding and did not witness the occasion. I found out after 16 years of marriage and divorce that my grandmother had shared a concern and prophecy with my mother about my dating and marrying the man I did. My grandmother had literally told my mother that my husband was going to hurt me and that he had a secret that had not manifested itself to most, but that she could see it. In turn, my mother told her to stay out of my life and allow me to make my own choices, asking my grandmother to promise not to tell me.

My mother did not tell me about this promise she swore my grandmother to until she was told the reason for my divorcing my husband was in essence the very secret she asked to be kept from me. There are no words to describe how I felt once receiving knowledge of what my grandmother had discerned about my husband.

This same grandmother had a 4th grade education and told me several times in my late teens to not worry about the boys, but to get my college degree and marry a preacher and do the work of the ministry. Often, I stared at her in confusion, thinking "She doesn't know what she's talking about." Plus, I didn't see anything like that in my neighborhood or church, so it was also foreign. I did witness professional women who were teachers, nurses, etc., but most were single or married to lay men. What my grandmother spoke over my life was not only foreign, but incomprehensible for me.

Today, after 13 years of divorce and single parenting, walking in the knowledge of Christ, 3 ½ earned degrees, plus 18 hours of a MBA, and www.ResourceWoman.com I can say God has been very good to me. The cliché, *"Your misery is your ministry"* is touché in my life. I have had the enormous and humbling opportunities to undergird, counsel, and teach so many individuals the truth about waiting on God's timing, especially in choosing mates. The emotional pain I experienced, I would not wish on my worst enemy. In my singleness, I still desire a life partner, but only the one God has specifically fashioned for me. I'm delighting myself in the Lord and know He will give me the desires of my heart. *I will not settle for anything but God's best in my life*!

As a closing note to everyone reading this book, and more intimately, this chapter- I pray you find a piece, part of the testimonies to deliver you out of a toxic wrong situation that God doesn't ordain you to be in, or strengthened a marriage or relationship that has gone bad but could be right in God. For those who have gotten discouraged or weary in waiting, please do not settle for less in choosing a mate. Occupy yourselves productively while waiting on God, He will show up in your life right on time.

Dear Lord, I Think I Married The Wrong Person

What I learned by not waiting on God's timing for a mate.

Please READ each reference scripture which support my statements.

- *To want only what God wants for me (Jeremiah 29:11)*

- *To acknowledge God in all my ways and* **KNOW** *He will direct my path.(Proverbs 3:6)*

- *Know that every good and perfect gift comes from God, and that the enemy of hell has a perpetrator to mimic what is true. (James 1:17; Matthew 7:11; John 8:44)*

- *To know that people are not always what they appear to be. Whether they sit in the church house or not (I Corinthians 2:14; I John 4:2)*

- *What may look like God, sound like God, isn't always God... Do a spirit check!!! (I John 4:1-6)*

- *To be anxious for NOTHING... (Philippians 4:6)*

- *The cost of disobedience is expensive (I Samuel 15:22)*

- *God is not obligated to fix and bless what He did not ordain and will root it up no matter how long it has existed (Matthew 15:13).*

- *TO WAIT ON GOD! (Psalm 27:14)*

~Bobbie Clark-Alexande

Tennie Tyler

Is a writer and motivational speaker. She has studied Psychology and Sociology at Texas A&M University-Commerce. Tennie enjoys reading a wide range of novels, writing and participating in family activities. Her passion for literature over the years has given way to cultivating her talents for writing and she draws on her own life experiences when writing which not only provides healing but also has developed her God given gifts to help others in their walk with Christ.

She is currently working on her next project a Christian book about trusting God, and continues working on a Christian fiction piece centered on aggregation of soul salvation, restored faith and agape love.

Tennie's motto is to *"Trust God until the last drop"*; the last drop symbolizes the never ending flow of the blood of Jesus that is a gateway to our Sovereign God.

Tennie currently resides in the Dallas, TX area with her two sons, and actively attends church nearby. She is an avid computer gamer and also loves to entertain family and friends with her own brand of southern hospitality.

Dear Lord, I Think I Married The Wrong Person

You can contact Tennie at:
UnitedWeStand_Steadfast@yahoo.com
www.facebook.com/SteadfastSheRemains
www.twitter.com/TennieT

Dear Lord, I Think I Married The Wrong Person

Jesus Loves Me This This I Know!

I have known of the Lord since I was a little girl and remember spending majority of my childhood in church. One of my favorite songs growing up was "Jesus loves me! This I know, For the Bible tells me so;" but I had no idea that one day, the true meaning of those words would be translated to me during a very desolate time in my life. I was twenty six years old and 3 months pregnant with our second son, the night my husband came home late and announced that our time was up and he was leaving. At that moment everything I learned at church went out of the window…

The Process: "Oh he thinks he's slick," I mumbled to myself, as I dressed the boys, in their hats and coats to go to daycare. December 2, 2009, Wednesday morning, the weather was fair, but not nearly cold enough for a jacket in this Texas weather. Thinking *how could he tell me at the last minute that the child support hearing is today, and that I did not have to come*? "Oh, I'm coming alright. I'm coming to every single case up until the day The Lord touches his heart and he changes his mind. There will not be a divorce, in Jesus name. Amen!"

I knew he would change his mind, because the Lord told me He would "restore my marriage." I remember the time the

Lord spoke to me like it was yesterday. I dropped my sons off at a church member's house and as I was leaving, one of the children of the family gave me a DVD and said I should watch it because I would really enjoy it. I went home and decided to watch the movie which was Tyler Perry's *Why did I get Married?* Play. There was a part in the play I related to and began to cry.

    I told myself at the beginning of our separation that every time I cry, to turn my tears of sorrow into tears of Praise and Worship. So I began to worship the Lord and after about an hour or so, I rested in His presence. Minutes later, I heard the voice of the Lord speak "I will restore your marriage." I was so shocked and excited the Lord would speak such a thing to me that I had to share it. Immediately I jumped up, grabbed my cellular phone and dialed the number to my mother in-law's phone. As soon as she answered, God advised me not to tell her yet. So I didn't.

    Waking up early just to get the kids to the daycare that my sister managed, by 6:30 am, was a challenge, especially now that I didn't have job to go to. I had just lost my job two days before and during this juncture sleep had become my best friend. But sleeping in was not an option if it meant my sister would find out I lost my job. It's enough they know I'm not with my husband, but they surely can't find out he's divorcing me and now I am without a job. *No way!* No way can they find out how much of a failure I am that I could not keep my man. I say "they," because if my sister knew, then my mother knew and then my brothers would find out and that just couldn't happen. In our household, we were taught, divorce was not an option, not as long as God is still around. *I will just pray and wait until this passes and he's back with me, just as the Lord promised! They won't ever have to know a thing.*

As I backed out of the drive way of my sister's daycare facility, I exhaled a sigh of relief, and thoughtfully congratulated myself for not letting off any signs of grief. Turning the steering wheel and heading downtown, I began to silently pray. I didn't feel right about today, but I continued in prayer. "Dear Lord, thank you Jesus for this day, for being my Father and for being with me. Thank you Lord that today will be another opportunity for my husband to receive a sign that we are supposed to be together."

Little did I know that when I returned to pick the boys up my sister would immediately know what I had experienced. Who knew that as I gave her a hug and silently wept in her embrace that she would discern her sister was experiencing heartache that was the result of a DIVORCE? Who knew she knew but never made mention and a whole year would pass and the matter would never come up until I could safely discuss the subject without unloading. *God is good.*

This was not our first time meeting at the courthouse concerning our divorce. Actually the first date was July 22, 2009. That was the day we met before the district Judge to have our divorce finalized, but little did my husband know that it wouldn't be happening then. I did not sign the divorce papers, but I did, however, file a written answer. Standing before the Judge that day, I watched as she subtly sized us up. After asking why I felt we shouldn't get a divorce I answered and said, "Because we have a family and have never attempted marital counseling. I believe that if we put forth effort we would be able to work out our differences."

Noticing the look of shock upon my husband's face from my response *he had no clue what had God told me nor did he know I still wanted to be with him*, I watched as she then asked him why he wanted to proceed with the divorce. He answered and said something like, "I have been a victim of domestic violence and we have reached a point of irreconcilable differences. I feel my life is in danger and do not want my children to witness such."

Although impressed with his conning answer on the spot, every part of me wanted to laugh out loud because I was shocked that he would use such a personal experience to attempt to sabotage our marriage. I glanced at him briefly and thought, "That was such a low blow." Even though I wanted to laugh, I couldn't because I was so terrified.

While waiting to be before the judge, I saw four couples have their divorces finalized even with a written answer. So I knew that we would be next, if God did not intervene. When the judge ordered court appointed marital counseling, I not only knew my husband was cringing inside, I also knew that God's promised would still stand. "I will restore your marriage." **I had won!**

During this time of my experience was very difficult. Being separated and waiting for the end result was very stressful to say the least. The constant rejection by this man I was praying and fasting for was painful and heart wrenching. Believing God's promise of restoration caused me to lay aside all pride and endure bad treatment, disrespect and so much demeaning that my self-esteem took a major hit. I could not understand for the life of me, how over night, he could go from being so loving towards me, to in a matter of weeks, evil, mean and hurtful. It was all a part of the enemy's plan I just hadn't realized it yet.

This day however, was a little different. Even though it was only a "child support" hearing, my spirit felt it was more. So I prayed. Everything was going smoothly until the child support hearing was complete and the judge announced we can now see the District Judge. Although my expression remained calm, I was coming apart. I screamed to myself, "NO, NOT THE DISTRICT JUDGE." At that moment I did not know what to do, and could not for the life of me, muster up a prayer.

Just a month ago I obeyed the Lord, who after telling me He would restore my marriage, months later told me to "Let go", so I did. After grieving and spending a little time with the Lord in prayer, I signed the papers. With the papers being signed, I knew seeing the District Judge, whom could finalize the divorce, today would be the day that either God's promise would stand or it meant that I missed what He told me altogether. **I had missed it!**

The Beginning: My ex-husband and I married on July 5, 2006 after dating for a little over two years. We knew each other from our church youth department, but became friends in high school when he was a freshman and I was a junior. We always had a great friendship bond when we were younger but I only viewed him as a friend or a little brother. Later I went to college and our friendship suppressed.

Years passed and we saw each other one night at the annual conference at the church we both attended. He saw me and immediately said, "Wow, you look so beautiful.", I blushed. I have never been the one to be impressed easily by compliments. My daddy told me every day how beautiful I was growing up and that was enough, but hearing it from him was different that day. It sounded genuine, real and innocent. He had my attention and I wanted to give him more. The next day I called him at his parents' residence and gave his younger brother my number to give him.

We began dating and fell madly in love with each other, literally and rather quickly. Three months in, he professed his love for me, at the time I was still unsure of, on my end. Shortly thereafter, we declared that the Beyonce's hit song *Dangerously in Love* was our theme song. Looking back now, that sounds a little crazy, which is why *Crazy in Love* was my special song for him. Ironically both songs befitting as they were signaled the upcoming troubles. God is a jealous God and no one should come before Him.

We became inseparable... He wanted to do everything with me and for me and I gravitated towards his affection so much that it became a crutch. I stopped hanging out with friends and everything was centered on him and our relationship. Months of dating crept into a year and a year into two years. We both were believers, attended church regularly and had a relationship with God. Our desire to please the Lord was of priority, but after constant time with each other, our desire to please one another and our flesh succeeded. We were in love with each other and wanted to make love without feeling guilty.

> *When our desire to get something or someone comes before the desire of God's will, we tend to compromise our character and integrity and lose focus. When we gain anyone or anything by compromising our love for God, it's not near worth what we compromised because we will eventually lose it. God's love is everlasting, not worth compromising for even a moment.*

We talked about marriage, but us getting married was not definite. I wanted to marry this man and my need for him created a sense of desperation. I knew he loved me and in my mind, if I played my cards right I would be married in no time. I can say this without feeling embarrassed or ashamed, because when I was able to own up to my actions and the horrible decisions I made it was then healing and deliverance came.

Five weeks prior to the day we married he proposed to me. We immediately announced to our families we were engaged and were busy making wedding plans. Those wedding plans were halted when just two weeks later I saw a pink line. I guess we were the only ones happy about the news of a baby, because the tension became heavy. No one was agreeing on anything and we both became frustrated and decided to just elope. Sounds romantic doesn't it? *Not!* The night we got married we were having a meeting with our pastors who were now my in-laws and the already tensed atmosphere became un-conducive and combusted. I was hormonal and mad at everyone. We went home to the apartment that I once lived in alone and we didn't even consecrate our marriage, which was a silent yet mutual decision we made. A blind man would have known we made a mistake at this point, but we kept on trucking.

I should have been excited, happy and surrounded by girlfriends and family as I prepared for the biggest day of my life. Instead I was snacking on crackers to ease my nausea and constantly re-assuring myself that it would all be better after we said our vows. I told myself, "I would have him and he would have me." I also believed that with this step we took we would no longer have to worry about nosey and controlling family members making decisions for us that we should be making ourselves.

Manipulation had led to a premature proposal, and a premature marriage, due to an un-expected pregnancy and unsupportive family. We weren't even married a year before another woman was in the picture. This was the moment I wanted to believe I knew I made a mistake, but truthfully I knew sooner. July 5, 2006, the day we married, I woke up anxious, nervous and sick to my stomach. I was 8 weeks pregnant, but that was only part of the reason I was sick. I was going to the courthouse to marry the man of my dreams behind both our families back, rather than the church we both were members of. I remember asking him on that day was he sure I was his wife and he said he was. I asked him how he knew and he stated because he prayed and the Lord told him. Still unsure but because of his response I was a bit relieved.

Dear Lord, I Think I Married The Wrong Person

After the first incident with another woman, I lost all trust but decided to stick it out. He begged and pleaded for me to stay. I knew I wasn't going to leave, but I was beyond hurt. Who knew that hurt would get worse? I gave him an ultimatum, either we go to marital counseling or I'm leaving. Initially he was adamantly against counseling stating he didn't need people pointing the finger at him for the wrong he did. I argued that he wasn't the only culprit in the relationship and that obviously I had areas for improving as well. He then gave in but never seriously pursued counseling.

He did however, do everything he could to regain the trust I had for him and I have to give it to him he worked pretty hard. For example, he would call while he was at the office to re-assure me when he had to work late, and then come straight home. He had even become more romantic and affectionate, which where things I used to complain about. After a year or so of this good behavior, things returned back to normal. There was peace in our home and I didn't mind being his wife now. I in fact, loved him more attributed to this amazing obstacle we were able to overcome.

We conceived a 2nd child. During this time in our life we were very active in church me more so than him due to my responsibilities. This season of working in the Kingdom, brought me out of the club and away from drinking alcohol which were some of the things we did together as husband and wife. Drinking had become a major vice for the both of us especially me. When he cheated the first time, rather than turn to God in prayer I begin to drown my pain in alcohol and going out. That was my way of covering up pain, insecurities and secretly getting back at him.

I would find myself going out and drinking every weekend leaving him at home with our son. Although he never complained and even joked that he liked me coming home drunk, I knew my motives were wrong and was going in a downward spiral, until I was asked to do certain things to help out at church. When I adjusted my focus to God and became more active in the church, conviction of the way I was living kicked in and my desires changed. His didn't. He continued to drink and go out but instead of doing those things with me, he began to do with co-workers and friends.

Once again another woman was involved.

At the time I was about 8 weeks pregnant and the stress of the news affected not only me, but our unborn child. After hours and hours of arguing and crying, I finally went to sleep. The next morning I woke up and me and my son's clothes, *who were sleeping with me that night,* were partially covered in blood. I panicked and ran to the couch where my husband was sleeping and announced that I thought we'd lost the baby. We went to the emergency room and despite the large amount of blood loss the doctor was able to see the baby's heartbeat. I went home the same day with doctors' orders to take it easy.

When we went home, he did everything he could to stay on my good side, hence the news of the other woman. The next day he went to work and did not come home until 5 in the morning. Despite the doctor's orders I lost all cool and harmed him physically, throwing punches back to back that all landed. He allowed me to without out making any attempt to stop me and after I exerted all my energy, he looked helplessly at me and apologized. He denied any unfaithful activity took place and begged me to believe him. Emotionally drained, confused and hurt, I fell asleep in his arms. A few cloudy days of nothing went by, and Friday came, August 8, 2008 or 8-8-8. I have to mark this day, because this was the day he "left". At the time I didn't realize, but this day marked "new beginnings".

I went through a very emotional and unhealthy pregnancy, that ended with me spending the last 2 ½ months on bed rest in the hospital under constant care. The whole time I was pregnant, all I wanted was to have the baby and rid any reminder of him from my life and body. I thought to myself *when I deliver our son, I won't have this connection I feel to him anymore, and then I can finally get over him.* That wasn't even close to the case.

One day after as I was nursing my youngest, I was looking at a pastor on television and he spoke on Faith vs. Trust and my heart changed. My desire changed from moving on and letting go to trusting and believing. I spent months fasting and believing in God for my husband to return home, saved and delivered. I realized that us ending so suddenly was an attack of the enemy and decided I would declare the victory in my marriage and over his life.

A few weeks after our son was born, I learned of the other woman he'd built a relationship with since our separation. I was confused, because he kept telling me he just needed some time away, that he still loved me and did not want to end our marriage. At the time of the news, we were still "husband and wife" just in different living quarters, so this information was very unsettling. This time I didn't panic, because honestly, I wasn't shocked. I knew there was always the possibility of someone else since we were living separately and he was not living a saved life. So I prayed!

The Destiny: I remember sitting up in bed reading when he called me and confessed that he was involved with another woman and would be going through with the divorce. As I hung up the phone, I leaned my head back on my headboard, closed my eyes and calmly said to the Lord, "What am I going to do?" At that moment the Lord spoke to me for the first time in my life and He said **"Trust me!"**, without shedding one tear, I smiled and a peace like no other covered me like a mantel. Since that day, I have been putting my trust in Him. With every trial, tribulation, and every storm, He has seen me through. With each victory has come strength and wisdom; my level of faith has been on a constant incline.

I eventually received complete healing and became one with the FATHER and with that the Lord fixed my situation *by dealing with me;* my heart and my mind. I evolved to a point where He knew I would be obedient and when He knew I was ready, He spoke to me to let go. I remember that day like it was yesterday.

When I heard the Holy Spirit say "Let go," I cried and grieved because I knew I had to obey this Man that had finally become the head of my life.

I also grasped the understanding that my experience was not intended to reflect how bad of a person my ex-husband was, he was only a pawn (Ephesians 6:12) being used by the enemy. What I experienced was what the enemy used as an attack method to destroy me. All the enemy wants to do is destroy our lives, our purpose and ultimately our destiny (1 Peter 5:8) and he will use whomever and whatever he can, to do just that. During the time of my marital problems I should have remained sober and prayerful, in order to remain strong to battle the enemy. Instead, my spiritual weakness coupled with hurt, caused me to battle the enemy (a spiritual being) in the flesh. Later, during my separation I realized the power of prayer and faith, although, at that point, the damage had already been done.

Even though the damage had been done and my marriage was over, it's not over until God says it over and His over doesn't end in tragedy but in Victory (2 Corinthians 2:14). With a new found relationship with my heavenly Father and knowledge of prayer and it's powerful affects, I was able to conquer the enemy and overcome the battle in defeat (Luke 10:19). My marriage ended but my life didn't, which was the enemies main goal. What I have instead is a relationship with God, which is His ultimate desire. He wants eternal life for all His children and eternal life is found through Him.

When the divorce was finalized my faith reached an all-time low. I was disappointed beyond belief. All three times the Lord spoke to me throughout this process, I was very close to Him and I was sure of the clarity of His words. God speaking to me and me believing increased my faith and when my marriage was not restored but ended, I lost trust in the Lord. For a brief moment I thought everything I believed in was not real and was a complete hoax. How could I clearly hear the voice of the Lord and it not come to pass. As I angrily searched the bible for answers I ran into Isaiah 46:11b "yea, I have spoken it, I will also bring it to pass; I have purposed it, I will also do it." That means that if God did indeed speak what I believed him to speak at that time, it will without a shadow of a doubt come to pass. Does it look like it will come to pass? Absolutely not!

His Word Settles It! Since then I have learned from the word of God, as a believer we must have a combination of Faith and Trust. Faith to believe God's words are true and trust in Him that He is able to carry out His promise, IF He so chooses. That trust should be extended even if He decides not to or if He changes His mind. Shadrach, Meshach and Abednego expressed their trust and faith in God in Daniel 3:17. The three brothers declared "If" when they spoke of God's ability to deliver them. Their faith said He "will" deliver them but from the beginning they answered and said "If it be so."

Dear Lord, I Think I Married The Wrong Person

When we focus more on having faith for the things we want rather than trusting His will for our lives, it will lead us off track. Why? Because we were created for Him and to give Him glory not ourselves. God loves to reveal His glory to us and through us and He can't do that if we interfere and attempt to do it on our own. We find ourselves in alignment and reaping blessings when we say no to ourselves but yes to Him. His will is for us to have a desire to please Him and He then releases the results of us doing so (Matthew 6:33).

Do I really want that promise to be fulfilled? Let's just say that IF it shall be so, it will be. Through it all, my desire is to please Him and have His will done in my life. IF that is His will for my life, I believe the Lord will adjust my heart and thoughts to line up with His. In the meantime I will continue to walk in purpose and ultimately accomplish the destiny He has for me. **My trust has now shifted from him to HIM!**

A year after our divorce when the tension between my ex-husband and I subsided, we had a very lengthy discussion. He initiated the conversation after we shared a kiss at our sons' 2nd and 4th birthday party. We talked about all the mistakes made in our marriage and he confessed the he wished he could go back and handle things differently. After sharing good times and some bad, we both discovered the biggest mistake made was our timing. Neither one us were ready for marriage and indeed entered into our union rashly. He asked me could I ever see myself with him again and I told him "We could never repair the damage that had been done and I did not."

Dear Lord, I Think I Married The Wrong Person

Since then, our parent partnership/friendship has been on the same constant rollercoaster our marriage was once on. My desire to be with him and the restoration of our marriage cease to exist and the change of my heart and his would certainly be a miracle.

There are a heap of things I would have done differently, and that begins with seeking the Lord first about my husband. Ensuring with prayer the man I was dating and falling in love with is doubtlessly my husband and then *WAITING* for a response. I would have kept the Lord first rather than solely indulge in a love relationship with someone else and then successfully completed pre-marital counseling. I was in no way the perfect wife and made countless decisions, of which assisted in our failed marriage.

My need for understanding was at its highest along with seeking the Lord in prayer before speaking and acting out in heated situations. Lastly and equally important, I would have never put so much of myself in another individual that I lose myself, and in the end when he still left and I knew he wasn't walking with a mind and heart of God, I would have LET THAT UNBELIEVING HUSBAND GO, immediately (1 Corinthians 7:15)

I have been divorced now for 2 years December 2nd and since that day I have started my walk in purpose. With all I went through in my marriage and the process leading to the divorce, I have a relationship with my Heavenly Father like never before. For that, I know everything that happened, did for a reason and was necessary. The Lord revealed to me, that the pain I endured in being rejected and abandoned by my husband was intended by the enemy to destroy me, but the Lord used this as an opportunity for me to learn to trust HIM. What the devil meant for bad, God turned it around for His good.

Now I can boldly say that it is better to trust in a God that will never leave nor forsake you, than man, any day (Hebrews 13:5), and with my trust in God, all good things will follow. My trust has always been in man, but when my ex-husband left, I was not working, a mother of one child and 3 months pregnant with another. I didn't know what to do, but God did (Proverbs 3:5, 6). He always provided and looking back, I see even through the tears and worry, provision was already made.

I married a man because I felt like I needed him. I needed him to love me, to make me happy and to make me feel good about myself. I was divorced by a man only to be left unloved, unhappy and even more insecure than I was before. All along everything I was looking for in "man" is found in God. He makes us complete, whole (Col. 2:10) and anything we enter a relationship with; we will leave with as well. A spouse is to help you be a better you that God has already created, not create you!

Sometimes we give human-beings too much power and although we like power, it becomes too much pressure to achieve goals beyond our measure. Only God is equipped to be God and only He can handle the pressure of our expectations, not man.

In Him, I have found love, confidence, purpose, healing, peace and a new beginning. I have peace knowing that all things, whether good or bad will work out for my benefit (Romans 8:28) and were constructed with purpose to conceive a better me as long as I love and obey Him! My purpose includes being an example of a Godly woman who applies faith to its highest dimension, believing in God to do the impossible in the most unfavorable situations.

My gift of faith coupled with my gift of teaching enables me to not only live by example but also to teach and exhort others to as well through motivational speaking. My experience allows me an opportunity to help someone else, by showing love, compassion and understanding to them in their time of need. Most of all I have another fair run to take all I have learned from mistakes and bad decisions of my past to be a better woman, mother, friend, servant and wife again someday, all while God receives the glory.

*My parents told me Jesus loves me, the bible told me Jesus loves me, but **now I know Jesus Loves me** and my complete trust remains in Him and Him alone!*

~Tennie Tyler

Dear Lord, I Think I Married The Wrong Person

Reverend Venora Gibbs - Chisolm

Is a Licensed and Ordained Minister, Founder and Senior Pastor of *Seeking God Ministries* in Norcross, Georgia. "Pastor Vee", as she is affectionately known, is dedicated to bringing the unadulterated word of God to the masses, without error or apology.

Pastor Vee believes in operating within the Five-Fold Ministry she has a Prophetic Anointing and has been called by God to be an Intercessor. When she is not traveling spreading the gospel, she dedicates her time to bringing the Word of God to the Prisons, Nursing Homes, and is actively involved in Community Outreach. Pastor Vee hold various degrees and has a successful Counseling Practice.

Pastor Vee is currently married and is the mother of an adult daughter Jovanna, and a four-legged son, Samson

For booking and additional information, please feel free to visit her website!

www.seeking-god.org

Sleeping With The Enemy

"For we do not wrestle against flesh and blood, but against principalities, against powers, against the rulers of the darkness of this age, against spiritual hosts of wickedness in the heavenly places." Ephesians 6:12 (NKJV)

I love my husband! I love him from the bottom of my heart, to the depth of my soul. I have never loved the way I love him! My husband really loves me. I never had to second-guess the magnitude of his love for me. I could feel it with every glance and touch. If someone had told me eight years ago, we would be separated, and possibly headed for divorce, I would have said they were crazy. Yet here we are.

When I met my husband I was in a "bad place." I had made the decision to divorce my first husband and I was in a lot of pain. At the time, I was a licensed and ordained minister, and was told that I would have to step down from my position of leadership. I hadn't always been saved and with a few words, I was cast out by my church. I had spent 12 of the 17 years married to a man incarcerated many miles away from me and there were no conjugal visits. He began to be emotionally and verbally abusive, and I wanted out, fast. I had a hard time believing God had brought me that far to leave me. But, there I was, in the world once again.

My husband is tall, dark, and handsome. I was standing in line at the Gas Station when he first walked up to me and introduced himself. He said, "I've seen you around. May I walk you home, I'm just asking." There was something about him that spoke to my very core. Maybe I could identify with his pain and brokenness. We spent the better part of the day talking and laughing. We had sex that night! I had been told I was out of order for seeking a divorce and had lost my position in the church, so I didn't feel I had anything else to lose. If you're going to do it, do it big!

I thought he would be my "transition" boyfriend. You know the one that would take me from my first husband, to my next husband. Well, within 30 days, he had moved in with me, and I had filed for divorce from my first husband.

We had been living together for a few months when I found out he was cheating. He may have been cheating from the beginning. Honestly, at that time, I didn't really care. I wanted him to cover his portion of the bills and everything else was pretty much a Non-Factor. As I look back, I was used to men cheating. I thought as long as he took care of me that was all that mattered.

I was with him about a year before my first husband signed the Divorce Papers. After being together about a year and a half, he asked me to marry him. He wanted to have a "clean slate" so he told me about his all his infidelity *so I thought* and I accepted. He told me he didn't want to wait, so we planned to get married the next month. It would just be the two of us going somewhere to elope. Little did I know things were about to go from awe to awful in half a heartbeat!

Dear Lord, I Think I Married The Wrong Person

Three days before we were to be married, he had a terrible accident at work and had to be rushed to the hospital. While at the hospital, I had his personal belongings, including his cell phone. When his phone rang, I answered it, assuming it was his family because the area code and exchange was the same. I had no idea the woman on the other end would change life as I knew it. She told me she was his "cousin", but something didn't feel right.

We postponed getting married and a month later, he had an accident in my car. Now, he told me he was going to see a friend who lived about 15 minutes away, but in reality, he was about three hours away heading to his hometown! I called the "cousin" to see if she was in the car with him. After speaking to her aunt for a few minutes, she let me know the woman was not his cousin and was pregnant by him. I thought someone hit me with a Bulldozer!

He was getting out of my house, one way or the other! He moved back to his hometown, and I was done with him for good! *At least that's what I thought.*

During his absence, I started finding my way back into God's favor. I had been through counseling and found a new church that didn't treat me as if I had "Leprosy." I had been redeemed and restored and I was on fire for God once again. I decided to sue him for damages to my vehicle and monies he owed me. He had taken my dignity and pride, he didn't have anything else coming. The lawsuit was selected by a popular television court show and there we were once again, face to face after so much time! I had not seen him in four months. After I exposed him on National Television, I thought he would NEVER speak to me again. *Yeah right!* No sooner as I was out of the taxi, he was calling and wanting to see me.

We had a wonderful night on the town and talked until the sun came up. He told me how sorry he was and how badly he wanted me back, not as a girlfriend, but as a wife. He knew I was back into position with God and the church so he agreed to my request of him to stop drinking and smoking marijuana, start attending church regularly, and going to Pre-Marital Counseling. I fell for it, hook, line and sinker! After all, I discovered somewhere along the line, I had fallen in love with him. It wasn't like or lust, it was a love that I had never experienced before.

Now, as we were preparing to be married, God showed me two visions. In the first vision, my husband was surrounded by demons. In the second, I saw our wedding. Well, do I really need to tell you what vision I ran with? Yeah, I ran with the wedding. Everything came together so effortlessly. I had no doubt God was moving everything into position. We were able to complete our counseling in one day because he was still living out of state.

My gown was originally $2000, but because it was the end of the year and I could fit the sample, I was able to purchase it for $100. We were able to have the church free of charge. We became husband and wife December 31, 2005. Everything was perfect and exactly as I had seen in the vision, everything except what really mattered, him. I had been disobedient, I didn't deal with the demons, and I would have to pay the price. I'm just glad I found favor in the eyes of God and didn't have to pay with my life.

He and I had been married for just three months when it started to decline. I had gone out of town for business, and he didn't wait for my plane to arrive at my destination before he was headed out of town to spend the night. He lied to me, so I can only assume he was with a woman.

He was used to working hard and I will never take that away from him. He would clean, cook, do the laundry and any and everything I could ever want. All he ever wanted was to see me happy. Any real joy I had experienced, always quickly diminished. I began to equate expensive gifts with him cheating. I never had an issue with him being physically or verbally abusive although the emotional abuse of his cheating was beating me down.

I couldn't understand how or when he had time to cheat, because we were together more than we were apart. I guess people find time for the things they want. During the course of our marriage, I was infected with a Sexually Transmitted Disease twice. He never stopped drinking and smoking per my request. I had already married him without him going to Rehabilitation, so it wasn't like I could make him go now. He was doing the most, and it was really getting on my nerves. Then and only then, I decided to do move according to what God had shown me. You already know, it was too late!

He had a seizure disorder. There were times he would function for long periods without having a seizure and then there were times they would be frequent. It may have been dependent on what (alcohol/drugs) was actually in or leaving his body. One day while in the bathroom, I heard him fall and begin to seize. I placed my hands on him and began to pray. I was praying from my spirit to the spirit. He flipped me into the tub and locked me in the bathroom. Finally, he heard me banging on the door, snapped out of it and let me out.

A few months later he had another seizure. Once again I laid my hands on him and began to pray in the Holy Ghost. He grabbed me by both my hands, looked me straight in my eyes and said, "I'm not going to let you destroy us!" I had never seen anything like that in my life. I felt as if I was stuck in the middle of a Stephen King movie. I was terrified to say the least!

God had spoken to me a long time ago regarding Spiritual Warfare. God told me, "There will be a time in your life when you will come face to face with your enemy. He will have one job, to steal your anointing. I have been preparing you for the appointed time." Immediately, those words came back to me. It was then, and only then, that I got ready for battle!

I was scared and had no idea what to expect, but I believed in God. I would get up every morning between five and six in the morning to pray. I would walk through my house and anoint my door jams. It was during this time, God called me to be an Intercessor. I prayed without ceasing, from my spirit to the heart of God.

One morning, my husband got up and started emptying the dishwasher and slamming cabinets and drawers while I was in the next room praying. I didn't stop. I kept on praying boldly and with authority and he retreated into the bedroom. I had enough. This wasn't my first time dealing with demons. However, I had never dealt with demons of this magnitude.

Soon I discovered that if I anointed the doors he couldn't come in the house. I was in the fight of my life! His drinking became heavier and he stayed out longer. But the demons were still there. I asked God why was it I didn't have power to cast out these demons but I could cast out others? He said, "Because you are now too close!"

Then one day we made love like we had never made love before and that was all it took. I let my guard down and satan caught me sleeping! The enemy knew where I was weak and used it to his advantage. How could this happen to me? I was a Woman of God; I paid my tithes, attended regular service, and taught His messages. When God spoke a word to me, I delivered it as I received it. How could God allow this to happen to me, had I not found favor in His sight?

I'll tell you how, because I did not listen to what God had told or shown me. *"Behold, to obey is better than sacrifice, And to heed than the fat of rams."* 1 Samuel 15:22 (partial) (NKJV)

The demons that were attached to him, had attached to me! I found out he had been having a relationship with a girl for over a year. The girl was a year younger than my daughter and her mother knew about it. The girl had lived right next door to us, so she and her mom knew he was married. Her mother claimed my husband told her we were divorced. *All she had to do was come by to check.*

Soon after he started lying every time his mouth opened and he began to steal money and jewelry from me. My solution to the problem was out of order! I quit my job, stopped cooking and cleaning, and to stopped making love to him. I did NOTHING all day, every day. He was miserable and I was happy.

A short time later, I met a young man over ten years my junior. He was fine, had a nice body and wanted me. It took no time for me to give my body to that man. One would have thought I couldn't spell "Saved!" I became disrespectful to my husband. I even stayed out all night with my lover and when my husband asked where I had been, I told him it wasn't his business. Sure, I felt guilty afterwards, but what was done, was done.

I hadn't just cheated I was having an affair right under my husband's nose. How could I allow this to happen to me? I saw the path I was on and it was all too familiar, I was on the path of destruction.

One day, my lover had asked me if he could attend church with me. OH NO! He couldn't possibly go to church with me, because they knew my husband. It was right then that it "clicked!" I heard God say to me "Here is a soul that you could have brought to the Kingdom, instead you choose to be in satan's playground." That was a serious "Reality Check" for me. Instead of being in position so God could use me for His glory and the advancement of His kingdom, I had failed at my assignment!

Dear Lord, I Think I Married The Wrong Person

I had made a mess of things. I was not the woman or wife God called me to be. I began to work on me from the inside out. I asked God to forgive me and my husband as well. I began to seek God diligently. During this time, God referred me to Genesis 2:21-24. Marriage was the first blessing God gave His people, and it should be revered. I was also taken back to Proverbs 31:10-31, because although I knew that scripture by heart, I had missed a key element. I began my healing process and was angry that I allowed myself to be in the position I was in. I knew better!

God used my husband to teach me obedience and submission. I did not know the true meaning of those words before I met him. God knew that if I would submit to him, I would be able to carry out my assignment. You may understand how hard it is to be obedient and submissive to someone whom you feel is unworthy. I began to reclaim my fire and strength. Things were falling back into place for me spiritually and professionally. My personal life was a different story. My daughter and husband were out of control. It was now time for me to do what I do best, go before the Throne of God! I went on a fast for seven days. I didn't let anything enter my mouth, because I had to be in place to hear from God. I had to truly be broken.

On the sixth day, I prayed for my daughter and my marriage. The very next day, my daughter informed me she was going back to school and needed me to complete some financial documents. No more than an hour later, my husband told me he was going back to his hometown, in another state. He would be leaving the coming weekend. I had mixed feelings, but he was sucking life out of me, so I had to let him go.

Dear Lord, I Think I Married The Wrong Person

My husband and I separated September 6, 2008. We speak civilly to each other for the most part and have even spent some time together. We have a wonderful time when we were together. Actually, while we were living together we rarely argued. I can count them all on one hand and they had to do with his infidelity.

He never thought I would have had an affair. To him I was the "Good Girl" and no matter what he dished out, I would take. He told me he counted on the fact that I loved him so much. However, he forgot that I loved me more than he ever could and enough was enough!

He shared with me that I broke his heart when I cheated on him. He knew it wasn't just sexual, but a relationship. He told me he couldn't handle it. It may sound selfish and mean but I wanted him to feel the same pain I had felt so many times. I can and will admit I was wrong on *so many levels*. I love my husband as I did when we first met and I miss him so much. The very first time I laid eyes on him and he spoke to me, my heart skipped a beat. I KNEW he was the one and that may have been the reason I slept with him that night.

God has used this time of our separation for His glory! Because I had gotten to a place of "brokenness," I was in position for elevation. God knew that I couldn't concentrate on Him and my husband at the same time, so hubby had to move. I had never been alone before and was uncertain of so many things. God began to give me scriptures to help me heal. The first scripture was Joshua 1:9 *"Have I not commanded you? Be strong and of good courage; do not be afraid, nor be dismayed, for the Lord your God is with you wherever you go."* I also began to meditate on Jeremiah 29:11-15, Psalm 63, Psalm91, and Psalm 119. I used my time wisely and waited in God.

Slowly but surely, I began to get my life right. I was granted my position in ministry and began to counsel couples. That in and of itself showed me God had a sense of humor! I had actually been on each side, the cheater and the cheated on. I had another testimony. God knew I was going to mess up and fail before I did. He will orchestrate things so that in the end, the glory is all His. I know that my husband's infidelity had nothing to do with me.

This is something I learned after our separation. While we were living together as husband and wife, I kept trying to figure out what I was doing wrong to make my husband seek another woman. He has demons he cannot begin to understand, and they were there before me. Now there is some distance between us, I can be the wife God called me to be. I pray for him and his deliverance. It's not easy to pray for someone you don't like and have probably wished dead. But, that's a sign of spiritual maturity.

God has began using me in ways I could've never imagined. My Ministry is thriving because of my dedication to God. He has opened doors and blessed me in ways that are not possible in the natural. I have had "Divorce Papers" in my Nightstand for almost two years, but I haven't sent them to him because God is saying "No, not yet!" God has the final say, and whatever it is, I can handle it.

See, I couldn't fully love my husband, because I didn't love myself. Although I had given my life to God, I allowed satan to remind me of my past, and tell me what I did and did not deserve. I will never let satan have power over me again. I refuse to allow a foothold to become a stronghold! See, all I did to Neal was bark orders and tell him he had to change to be with me. God has corrected me. It's not up to me to make him change. As his wife, it's my duty/obligation to pray for him so he can seek God to change.

I have learned that my love is supposed to be unconditional; the way God's love is for me. I had a list of requirements for my husband that Jesus may have had a hard time filling, and that's sad. God did not give me to him to be his mother, but his wife. Although the Bible tells us that a man is to love his wife as Christ loves the church, nowhere is it stated that a wife must love her husband. We are to honor and respect him, and that's not done by browbeating, fussing, and cussing. All the hell we raise, pushes them further away. As women, and especially Women of God, we have to be the change we desire to see in our husbands.

God has told me my marriage will be restored before the year is over. We recently spent some time together. I had a wonderful time and didn't want to come home without him. We have agreed to work on our marriage and to see each other twice a month. We are still living in different states. We speak on the phone each morning and night to pray for one another and our marriage. We should be renewing our vows before the end of the year. I am not making a move without hearing from God.

Dear Lord, I Think I Married The Wrong Person

I know I have to do what He tells me to do and move when He tells me to move. I believe I was created for my husband. In order for him to be the husband God has designed him to be, I have to be the wife I was called to be. I have to find balance within my ministry and my family. I thought as long as I was taking care of "God's Business" the rest would just fall into place, and I was wrong. Just as I have a responsibility to God and the church, I have an obligation to my husband.

Please consult God with every area concerning your current or upcoming marriage! In order for your marriage to be successful, God HAS to be the head.

Dear Lord, I Think I Married The Wrong Person

My Advice To You

❖ Before you run to the phone, take it to the "Throne!" People will not forget all the things you tell them concerning your spouse. To avoid them being treated differently or judged, keep your mouth closed! Unless you are being abused, keep others out of your marriage.

❖ Fast, Fast, and FAST! If you really need to hear from God, fast. It is in your brokenness that you will find answers and blessings.

❖ There is NOTHING that can happen in your marriage that you cannot recover from! We are imperfect humans, so mistakes will be made. Learn to forgive!

❖ Listen to your Spirit of Discernment! You have the gift for a reason! If something doesn't feel right, examine it. If you try a spirit by the spirit, you will know what the root of that spirit is (Light or Dark).

❖ Trust works both ways! If you feel the need to check your mate's cell phone, email, Facebook, Twitter, etc., your relationship is already in trouble.

❖ Date one another. Just because you're married, doesn't mean you have to stop dating each other. The same things you did to get your spouse are the same things you have to do to keep them.

❖ Speak KINDNESS and LIFE into your mate!

~Venora Gibbs-Chisolm

Dear Lord, I Think I Married The Wrong Person

Ayanna Lynnay

Ayanna's zest and zeal for the Lord is apparent in everything she does and to everyone who has been graced with her presence. Like many who have come to know the Lord, Ayanna had to first become victim to the ways of the world, before realizing that her life and more importantly, her soul, were worth much more than the value she had placed on them. Fighting through various early adulthood struggles and a life of misery and destructive behavior only proved to Ayanna, that she couldn't just duck and dodge through this life and expect to be victorious in the end. She made the life altering decision to hang up her gloves and reach out to Jesus Christ as her Lord and Savior. Needless to say, it was the best decision she had ever made. Now with a life dedicated to the Lord, she is transforming into the woman she never knew she could be and helping to transform other lives as well.

Formal ministry training at Jameson School of Ministry and Theology as well as practical ministry training taught by the Holy Ghost and by serving leadership, prepared and equipped her to go forth in what the Lord has called her to do. Blessed with wisdom, insight and a general love for the Lord and His people, she is a motivator & inspiration to many.

She co-founded Millennial Kingdom Ministries now known as *The Transformation Station* located in Millville, NJ in which she is the Pastor or Transformation Coach as she sometimes refers to herself. She is also the founder of *IGNITION the Youth Movement* where the lives of many youth are being transformed as they are learning what it takes to have a true intimate relationship with the Lord. November 2010 she started ChosenButterfly Publishing ~ *Where Books That Transforms Lives* are written and published.

Ayanna is the author of *Devil, Please I am Not Offended {Overcoming the Spirit of Offense}*. And has Co-Authored two books *When Sisters Speak; Life Lessons from Women in Ministry*, and *Dear Lord, I Think I Married the Wrong Person-Her Story*. The Lord has given Ayanna a plethora of book, play and even movie ideas all with the central theme of transformation.

Ayanna is a mother (natural, spiritual, and foster), ordained minister, mentor, author, book publisher, and so much more. But the title she is most thankful for is, Anointed servant of the Most High God.

For more information visit her on the web

www.cb-publishing.com   or   www.the-tstation.com

Or email her at Ayanna@the-tstation.com

Dear Lord, I Think I Married The Wrong Person

A Marriage Built On Sand Cannot Stand

When I got married 12 years ago I was not serving the Lord, nor did I go to church or even read the Bible. I say all of that because I strongly believe that if the foundation of something is not based on the Word of God, when trials and tribulations come it will not be able to stand.

Similar to the parable found in Matthew 7:25-27 *The rain came down, the streams rose, and the winds blew and beat against that house; yet it did not fall, because it had its foundation on the rock But everyone who hears these words of mine and does not put them into practice is like a foolish man who built his house on sand. The rain came down, the streams rose, and the winds blew and beat against that house, and it fell with a great crash."* The storms hit this marriage and because it was built on sand instead of the Rock it was not able to stand.

My Ex and I were first introduced by a mutual friend. She attended nursing school with me and had been in the Army with him. She called me one day to invite me to a cookout that she was having and told me she had this guy coming she wanted me to meet. I was 21 years old, wasn't seeing anyone at the time so I was like "Sure, Why not?"

She went on to describe him and everything she described sounded real good to my flesh. He had a good job, his own car, apartment, no girlfriend and no children and to add a cherry on top he wasn't half bad looking.

"Say no more! That's my husband." I blurted out. I had not even seen this guy or had any interaction with him but everything my friend was telling me about him was just what I felt like I needed and wanted.

Little did I know I had prophetically spoken something that surely came to pass. Of course I had not prayed or sought God because I was not there. I just briefly thought about all the bad relationships I had been in with drug dealers, people who cheated, lied, etc.; who basically had nothing to offer me and from the way this guy was being described he had what I was looking for.

I have to digress for a moment to tell you. I was 21 years old, was not serving the Lord so in actuality I had no clue what I wanted or needed in a mate, nor did I really know what I had to offer to a man. All I did know was I was tired of being in dead end relationships. So here I was plotting and planning to make this guy I had never even met my husband all because he seemed like a nice guy and was about something besides all of the drama and negativity I was used to.

Long story short we met and exchanged numbers. We talked on the phone for a few hours daily and it did not take long to see he too was broken. I found out that he had grown up in a dysfunctional home where he was verbally, emotionally and physically abused. As a result he had low self-esteem and also battled with insecurity, rejection and had a fear of failure.

Dear Lord, I Think I Married The Wrong Person

His issues were part of the reason he was not in a relationship. He had shut himself down from having close relationships with people and would just shut himself up in his dark gloomy apartment smoking cigarettes, drinking beer, and playing video games.

I too had *many* issues such as low self-esteem and self-worth and the way I dealt with my issues was by being in one broken short-term relationship after another. I never spent time with myself getting to know what made me tick. I did not realize my low self-esteem and lack of trust for men came from not having my father around.

As a little girl my father and I were very close and had a special bond but that all went down south when he turned to drugs in my adolescence years. Now instead of my daddy letting me know how special and beautiful I was, I turned to boys and eventually men to get that affirmation; even if it meant giving them my body. Out of the hurt and disappointment of no longer having my daddy around, I developed a hard "I don't care" attitude and could cut people off when I did not get my way.

Two broken people looking for love in all the wrong places; instead of looking to the Lord and allowing the Lord to work on us individually. We kind of just meshed together and seemed to fill the void and lack in each other.

We moved in together after dating for just a short time. Early on there were warning signs letting us know this is not the right relationship for either of us. We argued constantly. I did not understand him and he did not understand me. We both were as opposite as two people could get.

We never developed a friendship. We had nothing in common. We did not like any of the same things. We argued constantly and did not see eye to eye about anything. I belittled him and made him feel worse about himself and to be honest I did not value or respect him nor was I even in love with him.

Don't ask how or why we got married on November 6, 1999 because even a month before the wedding we were talking about calling the wedding and relationship off *My God, I wish we would have*. We both had gotten signs and nudges of warning from the Lord that we were not compatible and should not proceed any further but when you get comfortable even in dysfunction it is hard to leave.

It was the first night of my honeymoon that I knew without a shadow of a doubt that this marriage was a mistake. It was almost like wearing blurry glasses and one day you clean them and can now see crystal clear. That was how I felt like "Oh my God, what did I do?" We both knew this was a toxic relationship and yet we ignored all warnings and had proudly proclaimed in front of 100 witnesses and God "We Do" now lying in bed in Jamaica we had no clue about the downward spiral our disobedience and ignoring the warnings of God would cost us.

Not long after the honeymoon the marriage took a horrific nosedive. I wanted to act like I wasn't married and that is exactly what I did. I stayed out as much as I wanted to. I started really drinking, drugging and even sleeping around. I was so lost and did not have a clue. Things got progressively worse. I was doing everything that I wanted to do but yet I was feeling unfilled. I was miserable on the inside and really did not want to be the person I was. I remember praying and saying "There has to be more to life than this." I later found out that my husband was praying for me as well.

April 7th, 2003 I had a road to Damascus experience. I was at the bar tossing back drinks living the married but still single life and later that night I went over to a girlfriend of mines house. She completely caught me off guard when she asked if I wanted to watch a church tape. I told her "NO, I am not into all that stuff."

Well she put it on anyway it was a preacher named Rita Twiggs and she was preaching at a Woman Thou Art Loosed Conference. To be honest I cannot recall what she was preaching that night because it bypassed my intellect and spoke right to my spirit. It was the most surreal experience and that night my eyes opened up. The dark cloud of depression lifted and gave way to light and love. For the first time in my life I realized the enemy had been trying to steal, kill and destroy me and my destiny, *a destiny that I never even knew I had*.

The change in me was so great my family and close friends thought I had lost my mind and to be honest I didn't care. Finally I had found that love, acceptance and confidence I was searching for, for so long in all the wrong places. My calling and the purpose the Lord had on my life begin to be revealed. I was so excited and surprised. I had no idea serving the Lord could be so wonderful and fulfilling! I just wish I could say the same about my marriage but sadly the downward spiral continued.

Once I got saved the whole family started going to church and the arguing and name calling stopped. The Lord dealt with me about my attitude and ungodly ways. The love and appreciation I had for the Lord made me want to please Him for the rest of my life and I knew I could not treat my husband the way I was treating him and still please God. But one thing I could not change was the fact I was not in love with him and felt no connection to him whatsoever. *I truly believe we never became one and that is why it was so easy to come undone…*

The Lord began to do a quick work in me and it wasn't long before I was doing Bible Studies and ministering to people. My husband was going forth in ministry as well but for whatever reason people did not really receive him (I later found out when a person knows the word but is not applying the Word there is no anointing and people don't feel anything that you are saying.) This began to put even more of a strain on us as old feelings of insecurity and failure started to resurrect in him.

I tried to encourage and motivate him. I prayed on, with, and for him. I spoke life into him which seemed to bud for a moment but would quickly fade and die off. He began to depend on me more and more and to be honest I started to resent that. I wanted my husband to be the man, who I as the wife, could depend on for wise counsel and to figure out our next move but instead the roles were reversed and he was always coming to and depending me.

Dear Lord, I Think I Married The Wrong Person

Our house was out of order and anything that is out of order just won't work. Because he battled with a fear of failure it made him not want to try anything that he could possibly fail at which meant he never initiated or tried anything. All of the main decisions for everything came down to me- which kept me in a state of feeling overwhelmed and truthfully at times angry.

People would often say I seemed to be wearing the pants in the relationship and in the ministry, this was *NOT* what I wanted but sadly he seemed to have no direction for himself, the marriage, or the ministry. To me, it seemed like it was easier for him to let me plan and execute everything. I wanted to be able to follow his lead but he was too busy trying to follow mine and because he battled with being fearful of failure he never stepped up or when he did step up he usually made such a big mess that I would have to pray for the Lord to hold my tongue and to help me not to get frustrated.

He was oblivious to anything that concerned me it was like he lived in a bubble world where he could act like failure did not exist. It was only recently that I learned women are created as *men's* helpmates and not the other way around. I am not saying men cannot help us but we were created to help them thus sometimes it may feel like we are doing everything and everything is on our shoulders but it is during those times we need to draw strength from the one who created us for these men. I did not know this during the marriage and that was one of the main reasons I would often feel angry and overwhelmed.

Meanwhile we lived separate lives. I stayed upstairs and he was downstairs. We were not affectionate with each other. It had been years since we kissed, we were barely intimate, and we just seemed to be drifting further and further apart. Neither one of us were in love and it showed. We were like two cordial roommates and nothing more.

The marriage did not bear any fruit. We were unable to have children; the church we started never grew. Our finances were destroyed because he had gotten fired from two of his jobs both times because patients complained about how rough he treated them. This bothered me not just because of the financial strain, but because he had different faces around me Vs when I wasn't around. People would tell me that he was an angry mean person when I wasn't around. Whenever I asked him about it, he would act as though he knew nothing about it.

Storms were hitting this marriage relentlessly and because we never had a true foundation we were being driven further and further apart. I was starting not to like him and as a result the feelings were mutual. I was absolutely miserable and was so tempted to walk away but it was my love and commitment for the Lord that would not allow me to just leave.

I stayed in constant prayer and even prayed for the Lord to allow me to die because I was against divorce and did not believe that was the path two believers should take. I repented time and time again for walking outside the Lord's will and ignoring the warnings and yet here I was still bound in marriage to a stranger I did not even like.

Dear Lord, I Think I Married The Wrong Person

    I bought and read books on marriage, watched and listened to CDs and DVDs on marriage, we went to marital counselors who suggested having date nights which we did but nothing seemed to join us together or make us appreciate each other. One time we went on a "date" out to dinner and we found ourselves playing the games on the placement out of boredom and having nothing to talk about.

    There were times I contemplated sitting myself down from ministry because I did not like the feelings of frustration and disgust I was feeling toward this situation. I felt like because of me making a vow while I was in the world (unsaved) now that I was in God I had received a death sentence. I am not exaggerating! That is how unhappy I was while I was married to him. He bored me beyond tears, we barely spoke to each other and not because of arguing but because we had nothing in common thus no conversation.. Even when we tried to conjure up something to talk about our conversations were about 5 minutes long. If anyone were listening to us they would think we were two strangers at the bus stop just making pleasant conversation.

    People often times have so much to say when they are not walking in your shoes. I have had people in ministry give me suggestions which I really did try to follow but what do you do when your Heart, Mind, Emotions are NOT there? What do you do when you rather die than get a divorce because you do not want to sin against God? What do you do when you can do nothing but cry because you put yourself in bondage? What do you do when you cannot stand when the person you married touches you? What do you do when you both try to become one but realize you are two puzzle pieces that simply were not meant to be connected? What do you do when your teenage daughter tells you they have never seen you in love and happy except with Jesus?

You Pray, Do what is Right & You Wait for the Lord to move and that is exactly what I had to do. I prayed for the Lord to help me to see my husband the way that He sees him, I prayed against my own negative thoughts and feelings, I prayed that the Lord would soften my heart toward my husband, I prayed the Lord would build him up to be the head and not the tail and I tried to do what was right.

In fairness he initially tried to make the marriage work. He had taken a lot from me early on and he hung in there. He could have walked out years earlier but he didn't; he hung around, stayed, and prayed. In hindsight I believe him sticking around was more because of not wanting to experience another failure and not because he was in love with me. He once told me the Lord said this marriage was going to work and to the outside it looked like it was. But upon closer examination a blind person could see we were roommates and nothing more. There are many people who stay in situations just like that and to be honest I probably would have too if he hadn't eventually walked away.

I knew I had to wait and trust the Lord because this marriage could not keep going down this road. In my heart I believed the Lord was going to have to move, either on us or on this marriage because He was not getting *any* glory out of it.

We had talked about separating and possibly "dating" each other while trying to build the foundation that we should have had in the beginning but before we could separate amicably he left the house for a few days without notice. He did this twice, both times during the weekend; which left me to unexpectedly have to uphold the ministry and handle the questions from those around. Once again this was another setback in my respect for him and something else that kept me praying and begging God to move.

I have been through some hellish situations and as a result toughness developed, but unfortunately the same could not be said about my Ex. He had been through some horrible situations as well but instead of strength he developed self-pity. A 'woe is me' spirit and it really, really made me upset. I cannot express to you enough how we were in no way jointly fit. Instead of our individual strengths and weaknesses complimenting each other they were a strong force of contradiction; all we did was clash and sound like clanging cymbals.

The final storm hit the marriage in an unexpected way. We separated the same day we performed a baptism for a young man who had been coming to our church. I had been working all night only to come home and once again find the weight of the ministry on my shoulders. There were some things that needed to be done for the young man's baptism that my ex was supposed to do it but messed everything up. Out of tiredness and frustration I told him "I think we just need to separate." He told me "Fine, I will have my things packed and I will be out of the house by tonight." He did just that, he packed his clothes, left and I never heard from him again. Ironically the only thing that he did not take was his church clothes.

From the time he left he refused any contact with me or my daughter who called him dad for over 13 years, he refused to pay any money toward the bills we jointly accumulated and owed, he changed my daughter and my insurance without saying a word {I found out when I attempted to make a doctor's appointment.} I had to fall to my knees and ask the Lord to HELP me and I wasn't asking for help to pay my bills but to help me not to hate my ex. I could feel the bitterness and hatred bubbling up on the inside because to me it was no reason to be nasty to one another. I felt like *Hey it didn't work it didn't work.* We could never say God did not warn us ahead of time not to marry but we both overrode the warnings of the Holy Spirit and now were suffering the consequence.

Out of hurt, frustration, anger or whatever other feelings he was feeling, he gave me his behind to kiss and has tried to financially hurt me and my daughter in any way that he could; including hiring one of the most expensive divorce lawyers in our area to represent him *The Lord told me not to even hire a lawyer but to trust Him, and I do!* Despite all that my ex has done or hasn't done during this time the Lord has shown me *He* is my provider and He has taken very good care of me!

I am not going to say it has been easy because it hasn't but then again walking by faith is never easy it goes against our desire to know how things are going to work out and takes away our control of a situation. We just have to KNOW God, know ALL things are going to work out for the good and HOLD on to the Lord's unchanging hand no matter how rocky the waters become.

I think it was an accumulation of the years of misery this marriage went through that when my ex finally left he thought to himself he was not going to look back and he has not looked back. Once he walked out and was gone for months without any contact, I knew in my heart this marriage was finally over and I was free to move on. After months of no contact, no financial support I filed for divorce to put an end to something that should have never had a beginning.

Reconciliation was never an option due to his refusal to make or accept any contact from me. If we would have talked and conversed there may have been a chance for reconciliation but that never happened. He changed his phone number, changed his address and basically in the course of one night disappeared out of my life never to be heard from again.

In the beginning I was upset, angry and hurt at the way he was handling himself considering the demise of this marriage was a result of *both* of us and the fact we were both professed to be Christians should have prevented this from becoming ugly. Just goes to show being equally yoked is not just saved vs. unsaved but can also mean you are at different levels spiritually, emotionally, intellectually, etc. To make it simple you don't see eye to eye and are walking in two different directions. I have found the more unequally yoked you are the more difficult it is to become one.

Dear Lord, I Think I Married The Wrong Person

I feel at peace with moving forward with the divorce based on the scripture 1 Corinthians 7:15 ~ *But if the unbeliever leaves, let it be so. The brother or the sister is not bound in such circumstances; God has called us to live in peace.* I am sure people will ask how can I say he is now an unbeliever especially since he prayed for me when I wasn't walking in the will of God and my answer is based on Ezekiel 18 which talks about how if we turn from doing the wrong things and begin to do right we will be rewarded but if we turn from doing the right things and begin to do evil we will suffer for that. It is not good enough for us to do right a couple of times and then turn to do evil. No matter how hard it may seem we cannot faint in well doing. Of course in order for this to be done a person has to *be in* and *remain in* Christ. Despite how we may feel at times the Lord always gives us the strength to endure and to continue to do what is right despite what's wrong around us.

Even though my former husband did a lot of right things in the beginning, in the end he turned from doing right and started doing evil. He has made his feelings his god and is following their lead instead of being led by the Spirit of God. *For those who are led by the Spirit of God are the children of God. Romans 8:14* this is why I say he is an unbeliever. A true believer would not be able to live in a harden heart state and persist in doing wrong. Since the unbeliever has left and walked away from his husband, father, and Pastoral responsibilities and has continued to stay gone, I am no longer bound to him.

It is funny how our prayers get answered sometimes. We want them to be answered in a way that causes no pain and does not feel uncomfortable but most of the time it does not work out that way. My biggest regret in all of this? My daughter being caught in the middle. She was close to him for the majority of her life and when he walked away from this marriage he willfully walked away from her. I would have never interfered with their relationship but the way things played out I didn't have to; he eliminated himself from her life. That hurts.

Was I perfect? Far from it, but one thing is for sure I have always tried to follow the leading of the Holy Spirit to get my wrongs right even when it meant humbling myself and apologizing for my many errors, short comings and deliberate sins. Prior to filing and even during the divorce process I made numerous calls, emails and texts asking for him to get in contact with me so we could talk if not as husband and wife at least as brother and sister in Christ all to no avail all. His heart is harden not only against me but also against the Word of God and for that I can't be upset, I actually feel sorry for him and I do pray for him.

At this point I feel at peace. I believe we did all that we could do considering our individual issues and where we were at in God. The storms were just too great for us. Not God, but for *us*… I am not afraid or ashamed to admit our faith, commitment and knowledge of God were not strong enough to sustain this marriage that was formed in sin and to make it work.

It would have taken both of us wanting to please the Lord, holding on to His word at *all* times despite situations and circumstances, denying our own flesh, carrying our cross, and enduring to the end. I think the only way we could have done it is if we felt God ordained our marriage. Our marriage is a prime example of the hurt, pain and cost of disobedience. In life there are some mistakes and lessons that cost lives and others that cost marriages. All that was learned and gained during these fourteen years cost a marriage but it has also help shape me into the Woman of God I am.

This marriage taught me how to pray and to wait on God. It taught me how to have self-control and patience. It taught me to trust God even when the situation seems helpless. It taught me about me and showed me the areas I needed healing and deliverance in. This marriage showed me what I really *needed* and wanted in a spouse as well as what I didn't want and certainly don't need. Despite how this marriage collapsed under pressure I am a strong believer that the Lord will take the ashes that we have made from our lives and still create something beautiful out of it.

Ironically as soon as my ex and I separated everything around me began to blossom. At this time I am going forth in all the Lord has entrusted me with concerning ministry and business. The ministry my ex-husband and I started underwent a metamorphosis and was renamed to *The Transformation Station*. Along with the name change the Lord gave me a new mandate, new vision and new means of implementation. The teenagers from IGNITION the youth movement (a youth group), I started in 2010 are growing leaps and bounds; they are learning to apply the principles of God to their lives and as a result living life for Christ. *ChosenButterfly Publishing* the publishing company the Lord had me to birth in 2010, is bringing forth fruit *{you are holding a piece of the fruit in your hand now!}* It is amazing what you can accomplish when your excessive unnecessary weight has been shaken off and you are now light and able to fly.

I had been with my ex for 14 years and had never lived the single life as a Christian. In the beginning I was almost fearful of being by myself. I worried about what would people say or think about me especially those in ministry, I worried about if I would ever find someone else, I worried if I would have enough money to maintain the lifestyle I was accustomed to living, and how would life be without some kind of companionship? Those unspiritual things did not stay my concern for long. I had to put my mind on spiritual things and get to the point of only being worried about what the Lord thought about me and what I needed to be doing for Him. Besides when I compare how happy I am now to how miserable I was before *It is worth everything that I had to lose in order to obtain the happiness and peace that I have since gained!*

Although right now I am content in being single I do want to remarry again but this time it would have to be with someone I am best friends with, no more roommates for me! He would have to be a man of vision who can lead in ministry and in our home. I have learned so many lessons and I await the opportunity to put to action all that I have learned!

This time of being by myself is allowing me to spend more time with the Lord discovering more about Him and more about me. I cannot stress the importance of knowing who you are and what you are called to do *before* getting involved in *any* relationship. Once we know who we are *in* God and what we are called to do *for* God we can start building our lives on the ROCK, with the people He intends for us to build with. It is only then we will be able to weather whatever storm comes our way and remain standing once the storm has passed.

Dear Lord, I Think I Married The Wrong Person

Some things to think about:

- You know you are not ready for marriage when you cannot hear the Lord's voice clearly and still have trouble obeying Him quickly.

- If you do not have any idea of where you are going in life you will not have any idea of who you need to take with you.

- When the foundation of a relationship is built on anything and everything *except* God's word you are bound to have lots of trouble.

- If you don't wait on God *before* marriage you will find yourself waiting on Him *during* and possibly *after* it.

- Marriage and companionship were designed for the Lord's purposes so don't get married for yours.

- It takes more than vows, sex and living together for the two to become one.

- When the Lord gives you a warning *not* to marry someone, do yourself and everyone else a favor and obey.

- Our mistakes and failures seem to turn our lives to ashes but if you give those ashes to the Lord He will give you beauty for them.

- How a person's relationship with the Lord is; is a good indication of how their relationship with you will be.

~Ayanna Lynnay

Dear Lord, I Think I Married The Wrong Person

Pastor Joanne Schlicher

is a woman with a very merciful and tender heart for people. She grew up in a dysfunctional, abusive, and oppressive home that left her with feelings of low self-esteem, which sent her on a spiral of poor decisions. A warped perception of love caused her to choose abusive and unhealthy relationships. But God took that weak, insecure little girl, and through a long series of trials and tribulations, she became a confidant, secure woman, with an inner strength that is unshakable, to the Glory of God!

Joanne has two sons and four grandsons. Her husband is a Pastor. She is a Registered Nurse. Her passion is Intercessory Prayer.

You can contact her

Via email: Angelgram0914@Yahoo.com

Or

Via Facebook: PastorJoanne Schlicher

Dear Lord, I Think I Married The Wrong Person

This is the Story Behind my Bling Bling

I must start my story in my childhood, because that is where my journey towards marrying the wrong person began. It was a hard, painful journey. Let me begin.

To say I grew up in a dysfunctional family would be an understatement. I was in survival mode and did not know there was any other way to live. With all respect to my earthly dad, I have to say that he was the cruelest man I have ever known. He was angry, controlling, verbally abusive, critical, and later in life I realized he was operating in a spirit of witchcraft. My mother was beautiful inside and out, a wonderful person, wife and mother, but she was the main target of his cruelty.

I had a sister 8 years older than myself, a brother 5 years younger than me. I was the middle child and the most hated by my daddy. I believe it was because I looked the most like my mother. She was American Indian with dark brown eyes and olive skin. I was the only child with dark skin and brown eyes.

All of the three children were victims along with my mother. My mother was emotionally torn down over the years by my daddy. I watched her try to commit suicide unsuccessfully several times. Finally, I watched her have a nervous breakdown. She was never the same. She knew God.

Dear Lord, I Think I Married The Wrong Person

This is my story of abuse... parts of my childhood are totally blocked from my memory, but I do remember certain things. My house growing up was a dark place, literally and spiritually. I lived in fear of my daddy. As hard as I tried I could not meet his expectations. Whatever I did was never good enough, and he would become angry. I remember him cursing and using the name of the Lord in vain. It offended my heart so much.

He told me how ugly I was, how I would never amount to anything, that I was a slut, and that I meant nothing to him. He never hugged me or said "I Love You." His words and actions left me weak, feeling ugly with no self-esteem or confidence.

I went to a small Baptist church with my sister all of my growing up. We walked 15 minutes to get there and we never missed a service. I was saved at that Church at age 13. It was at that Church that I met a boy that I thought was my Prince Charming. I was 17 years old. It was a case of good girl attracted to bad boy. No one understood it but it did not matter to me. I was in "Love".

He was so handsome, looked like Elvis Presley. When I saw his car come down my long driveway my heart would start to pound. I remember the smell of his hair... like Flex shampoo. He paid me lots of attention and I fell hook, line, and sinker. The sexual attraction was strong, but I held him off. He asked me to marry him when I was 18, and I gave him my virginity at that time. He would break up with me frequently, bring other beautiful girls to our Church, and sit right in front of me. My heart would crush.

A normal reaction would have been to not put up with this treatment, but remember I was weak and lacked confidence because of my daddy. My boyfriend dropped out of school, I graduated. He had no initiative to work. I graduated from Nursing School and began working.

My beautiful mother died when I was 20. I was living at home with my 15 year old brother and my cruel daddy. I was still in the same Church, loved God very much, but my emotions for this man overwhelmed and overrode any common or spiritual sense. I married my handsome guy, overlooking the fact that he was not working.

Love truly is blind. I was madly in love or so I thought, and also the fact that he was my first and only sexual partner, I felt that it was the right thing to marry him. We had hardly gotten home from our honeymoon, when the physical abuse began. My sister visited me, and I tried to hide the bruises. I would make excuses and say I bumped into the furniture.

It got increasingly and quickly worse. He would hold me down on the bed, choke me, spit in my face, kick and hit me. Once he punched my jaw so hard I literally saw stars. There is a bone in my jaw that remains sore to this day from that punch. I also had a broken tailbone that caused sciatic nerve pain. Then came the knives, guns, and the threats. I became terrified of him. While I was working he was staying out at night.

Dear Lord, I Think I Married The Wrong Person

One night I took a chance and called my brother and sister to come get me in the middle of the night. They did and I left hoping to never return but the nightmare did not end there. He stalked me for three years relentlessly. I was afraid for my life and continued to have sex with him out of fear.

The last time I saw him, I was in my car, and he was behind me chasing me in his car. He had a gun and intended to kill me. I got ahead of him, stopped and ran to a house, banged on the door. They let me in and called the police. The Police came and had him in the backseat of the their car, unknowing he had a gun in his boot. He kept begging and motioning for me to come and talk to him one last time. I did not. Suddenly a gunshot went off.

The police jumped out of the car, and realized that he had shot himself while sitting in the backseat. He left on a stretcher to an ambulance. His face was grey and that is the last time I ever saw him. But the fear of him was so deeply rooted in me that it took *many* years and *much* help from God to get over.

I was a nurse working at a hospital while all of this was going on. I learned early how to put on a front like everything was fine, while I felt like a scared little girl inside. Also, because of the tension in my home growing up, I had developed Irritable Bowel Syndrome, anxiety and panic disorder. I was having what I would later learn was panic attacks. They were severe.

After three years of being stalked and scared for my life, I met a man that felt like a rescuer to me. Keep in mind that I was weak and co-dependent at this time. God later changed that in a major way. We married quickly, and I carried a lot of baggage from the first marriage into the second. I was hanging onto my first marriage wedding pictures and in my messed up head felt that I would always love the man that was abusive.

Please understand when you are raised in abuse, it becomes a part of who you are. It can be a sick comfort zone. God would later deliver me from those mindsets of the devil. My second husband was a good man. He was ambitious, in college and after graduating, was a hard worker and provider. But something was very wrong, and I did not know what it was. I should be happy, why wasn't I? *It must be my fault*, I thought.

There was a subtle rejection at first but a woman knows when a man does not love her completely. I had a son, and two years later another son. Life was busy, but the feeling of lack in my marriage relationship was getting worse. I continued to go to Church, taking my sons with me but my husband did not attend. I loved God and was always aware He was with me.

My husband became more and more distant, our lives became separate. He was in his world and I was in mine with my two sons. My husband got into pornography very deeply during this time and I was not sure what he was doing while away from me. Excuse me for being real, but I was no prude and he got all the sex he needed from me and yet it did not seem to satisfy him.

Over time, he did not want to have sex with me, touch me, kiss me, or have contact with me at all, physical or emotional. I was so hurt deep inside. I tried everything to make him love me. I would do anything to seduce him into having sex with me, so I could feel loved for that period of time. SICK..... *Thank God I am Not that same woman today!*

Through long suffering in marriages, God was with me, teaching me to hear His voice in the Midnight hour. He taught me not by Book Knowledge, or in a Seminary, but trained me up by the Holy Ghost and the school of hard knocks. I had dreams as a child from the Lord and they intensified during these years of my life.

I learned the language of the Spirit of God. He spoke to me in Dreams and Visions. I learned to shut myself into a Prayer Closet and pray to my Heavenly Father who I loved and adored. It was the way I survived. It kept me from having a nervous breakdown, and it kept me out of a mental institution.

During this season of my life, God began to put a strength deep down inside of me that NO man could take away. He gave me self-confidence, delivered me from the words of my daddy that rang in my ears that I would not amount to anything... but I still wanted to cling onto this man that showed me no love. It is called Co-Dependence, and it is not healthy or of God.

My husband moved two states away to go to College and work. He did not take me or my sons with him. He would come to see us when he wanted. I was lonely when a wolf in sheep's clothing in the Church I was attending started paying me attention and I fell into it.

I was still legally married to my husband and told him what I had done. I was ashamed. He immediately called my family to announce what an adulteress I was and he filed for divorce. It was just the excuse to do what he wanted and make me look like the bad guy. I felt like a loser, but kept going for my sons' sake.

The divorce was final. The most difficult experience in all of this to me was the concern of how divorce would affect my sons. I wanted them to be secure and happy, no matter how I felt, or what sacrifice I would have to make. They did suffer from the pain of divorce, but God has and will take what the devil meant for their harm and use it for their good. Years later, I found out that he had been cheating the whole time we were married. *Go figure.*

One night after my second husband had left me and our two sons I was lying in my bed, with my heart shattered into a million pieces, when I had a Vision from the Lord. In the vision I saw words written on a Banner. It said **"When you get through this, NEVER forget the pain, because I will use you to help many hurting people."**

I know this is disgusting and may be hard to comprehend, but for 5 years after we divorced, I waited and prayed for that man to come back. I wanted our family unit together. I'm not a quitter! Finally It was September when I told the Lord I *needed* an answer... keep waiting on this man or let go and move on? I fasted that entire month. On the last day of September, God spoke to me *to release him and move on.*

It was THAT very night I met my third husband, standing at the foot of the stairs at the Church. He was My Angel sent to me by God, a gift to me to make up for all I had endured. We both knew immediately... he told me he loved me on our first date, and he really did. Twelve years later, he is still My Angel, still loves me unconditionally, and treats me like a Queen. God truly does *work ALL things together for our good.*

I *now* know who I am in God, I am Strong and Confident. I like to dress up in my Foo-Foo and Bling Bling to show the devil JUST how BEAUTIFUL I am despite all that I been through. In hindsight I would take nothing for all of the heartaches, trials, and tribulations I have endured in my life, for it was in all of these places and situations that God shaped me, changed my mindsets, and took me from a weak and needy little girl to a strong and confident woman.

I would say to anyone in an abusive marriage....**Get Out.** It will only get worse. God does not want you to be a Martyr or take abuse. He will protect you. I know the feeling of being afraid for your life, to the point of being afraid to leave. I have been there, believe me when I tell you to take that step out and God will cover you.

Ask God to show you His will concerning your marriage. He truly knows best. I want to say there is LIFE after divorce. When you are going through it, you feel that you can never love or trust again, but take it from someone that has been there....you will and *it will be worth it!*

~Don't judge me, THIS is the STORY behind my BLING-BLING

My Prayer

Father, I pray for every person that has read these words. Reach down deep into their hearts and minds and begin a healing process by the Power of God. Bind up the broken hearted, release those in the captivity of abusive marriages; strengthen the weak and faint of heart. Encourage and speak clarity and direction. Change Circumstances that are not of you. Open doors and do the impossible. Touch your daughters and sons with the sweet anointing of Your presence, and lead them safely to a new place, a fresh start, a second chance, In Jesus Name, I decree and I declare it to be so. Amen

~Pastor Joanne Schlicher

Dear Lord, I Think I Married The Wrong Person

Minister Tabitha M. Shannon

I live in Tampa Florida for nine years by way of Brooklyn, New York. I have a wonderful Husband named Eddie L Shannon. He is truly a man of God, and an Assistant Pastor at the church we currently attend, which is called, "Under the Blood House of Prayer a Deliverance Center" Pastor/founder, Pastor Barbara J. Neal and Co-Pastor Kathartis Neal. We have 3 Beautiful Children through his previous marriage, 1 daughter that I have adopted, (Julia Etienne), and 3 grandchildren.

I grew up in Brooklyn, N.Y. with my mom, dad, and 4 siblings. My dad was a city worker and my mom was a federal worker. They both worked hard and dreamed to raise us in a beautiful home in a suburb of Queens, N.Y. until there was a domestic violence case that opened the doors to a great deal of pain and hurt. In the mix of the separation, my siblings and I lived with my mom for about 4yrs. until she grew depressed and abandoned us. I worked very hard at 13, lied about my age so I could get a job, and had 2 jobs when I reached the age of 14.

I had been on the streets early in life, going from friend to friend houses to sleep, going through a process of being raped, drinking, drugs, promiscuous, depression, molested, abused, prostituted, gay, suicidal and so much more.

Dear Lord, I Think I Married The Wrong Person

Somehow, I decided to go to school and get my beauty license, and wind up owning 3 beauty salons in New York. I had my own apartment, and still had a drive to be somebody.

In March 2003, I moved to Florida after spending a few years taking care of my dad who went to be with Jesus because of renal failure. At the time, I was in the religious practice with Jehovah Witnesses. I had no intentions or plans of being in a church and yet in 2004 of Aug. God called me.

How do I know God called me? I was a sinner, and I had a family member that loved going to church, which she also came out here from N.Y. She wanted to go to a family-oriented church, so I had a friend whom I worked with that went to a church, and my plan was to bring her there, and I will fade out. God had a plan. She faded, and I found Jesus the Love of my life.

Six months later, I was in Minister Training class, and Our Lord and Savior Jesus Christ is still teaching me, as I go and do the command He has given us in Matthew Chapter 28:19-20
~Therefore go and make disciples of all nations, baptizing them in the name of the Father and of the Son and of the Holy Spirit, and teaching them to obey everything I have commanded you. And surely I am with you always, to the very end of the age."~

This, which brings about my Testimony of Dear God, I Think I married the wrong person! God Bless you all.....

Contact Minister Tabitha Shannon
Via e-mail: shannon.tabitha@gmail.com

Dear Lord, I Think I Married The Wrong Person

Taking the Lord at His Word

On July 29, 2005, I took a vow to marry a man name Reverend Parker. This was the second marriage I was going into, but my first Christian marriage or so I thought. We were both attending the same Church; A church that I had not even planned on being a part of. I started attending when a co-worker mentioned she attended a small family oriented church and I told a family member about it who wanted to go because she loved to play drums and sing. Once we started attending services, my family member faded but I wind up staying.

God started to really work on my heart, and changing my life. I received the Holy Ghost during bible study one Tuesday night and got Baptized in Jesus name in October of 2004. God was at this time doing a quick work in my life. He was showing me dreams and I was watching them come to past. This is something that blew my mind because I knew man, or a human being couldn't do what God was showing me.

Although I have a grandmother name Reverend Isabel Jessamy, who is the Pastor/founder for the Jessamy's Mission in Brooklyn, N.Y. and has been Pastoring for several years, I didn't know a lot about the Lord or how Christianity worked because I didn't grow up in the church.

My ex-husband and I became associates. Folks began telling me He was my husband and telling him I was his wife. We started working together on a church function, became friends, and started dating. I knew in my heart something was wrong.

Dear Lord, I Think I Married The Wrong Person

How? I had a dream and it was strange to me, but after this dream, I hear a small still voice state, "You made your bed, now you must lay in it." Why? Because I was having sex with this man, and it wasn't of God. I was shocked, but I was so convinced by the folks in the church, that this man was my husband. Folks stated, "God said this is your husband," and being a babe in Christ I believed every word. I continued to ignore God, and started listening to people.

I desperately wanted a companion. I had a lack of confidence and trust, and wanted to be loved, which caused fornication. There was no connection between us because we both were *in lust*, and not *in love*. By the time we married, we were two people living like roommates. I constantly felt like if you didn't need me then I wasn't interested. I didn't realize at the time that all I needed was to be completely sold out to God! As God continued to work in me I wanted to change and become this awesome wife that I had pictured in my head. I desired my husband to help me in the Ministry, show me what I needed to do, lead me, and guide me. I desired for him to pray with me as if he would pray with others.

That was what I anticipated when folks said, "God said he was your husband." We finally got married, and everything was good for about 6 months, but not the whole 5 years. For some reason, it felt like we were two people living as roommates still. I could not explain why I was feeling this way at that time and I had no idea that I would have to go through a process of being broken. I was so in love (I thought), I was at a point of being this great wife, was in Minister Training Class in 02/2005, God's Glory was all over me, I was getting all this attention from my Pastor at that time, I brought my new husband a new wardrobe, and so much more.

After two years of marriage, I found out simple things for an example; He was involved with this other women at the church for over 5 yrs., and she ask him was the rumor true about him and I dating, he gave her an excuse. Finally, after all of the foolishness, she left the church and never returned. I really liked that woman. She was sweet and was the Servant Leader of the Usher Board. My ex started showing signs of jealousy towards me. He would often say "You are not on my level" and when it was my turn to preach he would often leave me hanging by laughing at me, and saying things like, "You are going to freeze up there." He would not show any support towards me, but God was a constant supporter an encourager. My ex-husband always made fun of me or used the word of God to benefit him by making me look stupid. At that time, I didn't know as much of the Word as he knew it. I didn't know at the time that Romans 8:28 stated, *"And we know that all things work together for good to them that love God, to them who are then called according to his purpose"* I didn't know that Isaiah 54:17 stated, *"No weapon that is formed against thee shall prosper; and every tongue that shall rise against thee in judgment thou shalt condemn. This is the heritage of the servants of the Lord, and their righteousness is of me, saith the Lord.* God really had my back due to His love for me, He will never leaving me nor forsaking me, I didn't know that all I had to do was stand on Psalm 46:10 which stated, *Be still, and know that I am God: I will be exalted among the heathen, I will be exalted in the earth,* allowing God to fight my battle, being a Kings Kid, belonging to Royal Priest hood, and so much more.

Dear Lord, I Think I Married The Wrong Person

I cried often I started going to New York, Brooklyn a lot (running from problems) I was tired of feeling like a nobody. Being stepped on constantly, and told you are the one living in sin not him. I had so many questions such as: How is it that this man is a leader, and doesn't pray with his own wife? How is it that he preached one thing, and lived another? How is it that he doesn't see himself, but always pointing out my faults? How is it after 4 years were still living like roommates?

Sex was often denied, no date nights, no family time, etc. I couldn't understand it, but one day God showed me a dream. In the dream, we were at this hotel and I can look out to see the beach. As I turned around, I saw this Spanish man standing there. I asked him, "Where is my husband?" and he stated, "He is in the other room." I said, "No this is our room." I went into the other room and my husband was in the bed lying between two women. I was so angry, I walked out of there back into the room and the Spanish man jumped out the window. I woke up praying to the Lord, crying in secret, "Lord, what does this mean?"

Days passed by and I was in my bedroom laying out on my bed meditating. I heard this small still voice said, "Look at his phone," I automatically took the phone while he was in the shower, and saw texts from a women name Elder Doe. I said, "Lord she is an Elder- why would she be texting a married man about sex?" I was shocked, but at the end of the day, I waited and confronted him about the texts. He just stated, "Sorry won't do it anymore." No remorse, No sincerity, or nothing. I was so hurt, I called my Pastor. She stated, "If you don't go looking for anything, you won't find it." My heart was so broken, and my chest felt like it opened up and my heart fell to the floor. I didn't expect that type of answer from a woman I actually looked up to and yet I continued to fight for my marriage.

I got up one night to go to the rest room, about 2:00 am, and my husband was in the living room texting on the phone. He did not see me but I kept seeing him. I did not say anything. I started to believe God was showing me the truth. I was fighting God so long about different things he was showing me, because I didn't want to believe the truth. Instead, I was rebuking the enemy, I thought. I was beating myself up. I always stated, maybe if I do this, or maybe if I do that, but anytime a man is not what God chose for you it will not last.

I had no idea my husband was feeding lies to the Pastor and the woman he was dating at the church. How did I know that he was dating this woman? Well their relationship started to get reckless; they started a team date group and she was always with him, she cooked a large Thanksgiving dinner with him there. Her grandchildren called him granddad, They were caught in Wal-Mart together she had on PJ's and he was acting like a puppy in love they didn't even pay attention to their actions in public. I found out she was handling his money on the down low. I saw her give him money right in the church and she did not know I was sitting behind them, due to me coming in late.

God showed me a dream with her and him lying in a bed together. They were constantly locked in the finance room together- him and her. Folks acted as if they did not see it. All of a sudden, every time he preached, she was yelling out, "Preach, Rev!" Friends and Family day he stayed with her family. The Reverend Parker stated, he "has no plans in reconciling this marriage, and it is over." He wants no more of this marriage, and he is done. He took off his wedding ring as if he was already divorced. In addition, there was so much more that God was uncovering.

Regardless of that decision eventually, my ex-husband and I decided to relocate to save money. We were trying to work things out, but for some reason I felt like I needed to fix this marriage instead of waiting on God. We had a large communication problem with our marriage. What a large price I had to pay. We both decided to give the apartment complex a letter to let them know that we had decided to move. Then I received a phone call from the complex we were living at, and the leasing agent stated, "Oh we received a phone call from your husband stating, "He decided not to move." I stated, "Huh! I'll get back to you on this matter." I called him and he stated, "Yeah I decided we are not moving." (Mind you we have already paid this other apartment complex security deposit, and etc.)

I decided to just go back to my prayer closet and pray, leaving the situation in God's hands. On Saturday, I received a phone call from the Leasing agent (from the new complex that he said we was not moving to) stating, "I just received a phone call from your husband and he wanted to know when was ya'll moving date, so I will see you both on the first of March." I got so excited because I just knew God heard my prayers. On March 1, 2009, I was moving our things out of the old apartment and he was sick. I called my brother, Timothy, to come help, and he did. We were moving all day and I was so tired.

Dear Lord, I Think I Married The Wrong Person

As I sat down on the couch a small still voice stated, "Tabitha, go to the old apartment." I said, "Yeah because I need to clean it out etc." I went to the apartment, and my ex-husband had the locks changed. I was so discombobulated! I said, "Maybe I tried the wrong key." I tried it again, and none of the keys worked. I felt my anger rising, but the Spirit of the Lord started to minister to me. I was so hurt, upset, and was knocking on the door. He would not open it at all. Finally, I called the police, and they finally arrived. He open the door and I just said, "Let me just get my stuff." He let us in, and as I went into the bedroom, I felt a strange feeling. It was as if a woman was already there.

He had a bed in the room with a small TV set up. One side of the bed was set up in position of another person that was on that side. His side of the bed had his machine there. I walked into the bedroom and for some reason my attention was towards the bathroom. I said, "Lord I don't want to see." I left so fast, I did not take anything else. I got back to the house and cried like never before. I cried for days. My heart hurt so badly, and every time I walked into the church I felt like my chest opened and my heart fell on the floor. I could not do nothing but lift my hands up to God and cry out.

What a nightmare at that time. I called my Pastor and left on her answering machine that I moved out, due to what he had done. It's like he played a game, and made it look like I abandon him. All I felt was a pain in my heart that wouldn't go away! I kept on praying the prayer of Psalm 51:1-19 stated,

"Have mercy upon me, O God, according to thy loving-kindness: according unto the multitude of thy

tender mercies blot out my transgressions. Wash me thoroughly from mine iniquity, and cleanse me from my sin. For I acknowledge my transgressions: and my sin is ever before me. Against thee, thee only, have I sinned, and done this evil in thy sight: that thou mightest be justified when thou speakest, and be clear when thou Judgest. Behold, I was shapen in iniquity; and in sin did my mother conceive me. Behold, thou desirest truth in the inward parts: and in the hidden part thou shalt make me to know wisdom. Purge me with hyssop, and I shall be clean: wash me, and I shall be whiter than snow. Make me to hear joy and gladness; that the bones which thou hast broken may rejoice. Hide thy face from my sins, and blot out all mine iniquities. Create in me a clean heart, O God; and renew a right spirit within me. Cast me not away from thy presence; and take not thy holy spirit from me. Restore unto me the joy of thy salvation; and uphold me with thy free spirit. Then will I teach transgressors thy ways; and sinners shall be converted unto thee. Deliver me from bloodguiltiness, O God, thou God of my salvation: and my tongue shall sing aloud of thy righteousness. O Lord, open thou my lips; and my mouth shall shew forth thy praise. For thou desirest not sacrifice; else would I give it: thou delightest not in burnt offering. The sacrifices of God are a broken spirit: a broken and a contrite heart, O God, thou wilt not despise. Do good in thy good pleasure unto Zion: build thou the walls of Jerusalem. Then shalt thou be pleased with the sacrifices of righteousness, with burnt offering and whole burnt offering: then shall they offer bullocks upon thine altar."

then Psalms 61:1, *"Hear my cry, O God; attend unto my prayer."*

and ended with Ephesians 6:11, *"Put on the whole armour of God, that ye may be able to stand against the wiles of the devil."*

I called my prayer partner and we went into warfare! We cried out unto God, and continuously prayed day and night! In addition, when my Pastor told me, "She had to disconnect herself from me." She was the only one I knew spiritually. She took this dirty wretch of a woman into the Ministry, and taught me all that I knew (with love, tender-mercy, and kindness have I drawn thee). My heart was so destroyed because I felt like I had no one to help me.

Despite it all I still had hope for my marriage. I would send him e-mails; call him, text him, but no response. I was apologizing for anything I did in the marriage or asking him for us to get marriage counseling. I went to church once for Bible study and He took off his wedding ring. I was like "Wow, Lord, how can he take off his ring, are we not Married?"

A few days later, the other woman's brother came to me and said, "I went on a date with your husband and my sister." "Why did you say that?" I responded. He said, "It was three of us there, but I felt like I wasn't supposed to be there." Her brother knew too much information, which was true. Again, the pain rises up. I was at the church but it was as if everyone treated her as if she (the other women) was the wife, and I was just there.

Dear Lord, I Think I Married The Wrong Person

Labor Day Weekend (8/2009) would be my day of Jubilee. I was home packing clothes for the twins and myself. As I was packing, I heard the Spirit of the Lord say, "Bring your all white prayer cloth and your black dress." He told me "Ordination" I didn't understand, but I trusted Him! I arrived to the church. We all were standing outside waiting to leave. I decided to take my car, and as I was standing outside I was getting looks from people like "What is she doing here?" I saw his sister, the Prophetess, but she was with the other women. I said, "Lord." As I got in the car, and as I started driving the Lord started ministering to me He said, "The first shall be last and the Last shall be first."

Friday Night we had a service up there in Bradenton, Florida, and I started getting dressed. God was showing me my black and white but I being hardheaded wanted to wear pink and blue. As I walked into the place I saw all leaders wearing Black/White. The wives wore black/white including the woman he was seeing. My heart started racing, I started screaming on the inside as they gave out the service programs. There were three people getting ordain and one of them was my ex-husband.

I started praying, the spirit of the Lord spoke, "He is not the author of confusion, and He does everything in decency and in order." As they did the ordination they called up each wife or representative to stand behind the spouses. They were being ordained as Pastors. They called my ex-husband and the Prophetess to stand behind him, my heart went through the floor.

I walked quickly out of there with my twins when I got back to the room, the Spiritual Sister that I was sharing a room with automatically took the twins to the lobby and I went into the bathroom and cried. I felt like Hanna in the bible. I was crying out and my mouth was moving with no words. My insides felt like they were coming out. I was in dying need to kill my flesh. My heart was truly broken, and I was done. I said, "Lord, how is it that my leader doesn't see what you are showing me?" Help Lord, Help Lord. I prayed like never before and couldn't wait to get home. What an experience. I handled it the only way I knew how - I fasted and prayed so much I dropped a lot of weight. Everyone treated me as if I had leprosy. I felt so alone and it was so hard.

Despite it all, God never once left me. I knew that He was with me. I remember one day they were having Sunday Service and this particular day God just gave me peace, a peace that surpasses all understanding. I felt like I could fly throughout that place. I started to forgive folks and love on them even when they started throwing stones; I continued to give them bread. I was so at peace and my heart did not hurt anymore. I started loving on God more, and the more I found myself loving on Him, He was loving and restoring me. He reconciled me back to Him.

There was so much that went on in that marriage I knew that the marriage was not of God. Only God has brought me through. I learned that you can know the word from Genesis to Revelation but if it is not applied in your life, it is all a waste of time and hell will become your home. I learned how to become humble before the Lord and be meek with lowliness. One particular Sunday morning I was in service with my twins that were 18 months at the time, my mother from Brooklyn, my sister and her 3 children I looked around and the church was almost empty. The Pastor went to visit her son for Christmas, the praise team leader got married, and none of the other praise team members were there, so my ex-husband was trying to conduct Praise and Worship.

I stood up trying to get into the service and then all of a sudden- I begin to feel like I was being choked, couldn't sing, and couldn't get into Praise and Worship. This upset me a lot because praise and worship is my life. I felt like the Holy Spirit was trying to get my attention. I sat down and said, "Okay Lord, what is it?" The Spirit of the Lord said, "Go to the church you visited" (UTB). I looked back at my family and they all stood up at the same time as if they heard what the Lord said to me. I grabbed my stuff and we all left. That was the last time I attended that church! I felt so free...

There was so much more that happen in this marriage but I will need a whole book in order to tell it. (Smile) This was an experience that God allowed me to go through to draw me closer to Him even when I ignored His warnings, He still had mercy on me and His grace was in place. God allowed me to visit a church that I attend right now called UTB! I felt His presence, I felt like a strong tower, and God truly helped me, and continues to do so.

During this entire process, God kept me in His word. He began to show me who He was, things about myself, and how He operated. One day I was at home lying in my bed and had I just gotten off the phone with my prayer partner. I thought I was sleeping, but it was so real. The Spirit of the Lord was telling me about Dorcus (Tabitha) and had me to read Acts 9:36-42

"Now there was at Joppa a certain disciple named Tabitha, which by interpretation is called

Dear Lord, I Think I Married The Wrong Person

Dorcas: this woman was full of good works and alms deeds which she did. In addition, it came to pass in those days, that she was sick, and died: whom when they had washed, they laid her in an upper chamber. And forasmuch as Lydda was nigh to Joppa, and the disciples had heard that Peter was there, they sent unto him two men, desiring him that he would not delay to come to them. Then Peter arose and went with them. When he was come they brought him into the upper chamber: and all the widows stood by him weeping, and showing the coats and garments which Dorcas made, while she was with them. But Peter put them all forth, and kneeled down, and prayed; and turning him to the body said, Tabitha, arise. And she opened her eyes: and when she saw Peter, she sat up. And he gave her his hand, and lifted her up, and when he had called the saints and widows, presented her alive. And it was known throughout all Joppa; and many believed in the Lord.

Tabitha was God's Disciple and had a gift in making garments. I believe also Tabitha had a gift for hospitality due to the widows that loved her so. They heard Peter was in another town and they went to seek him out. The men told Peter the situation and Peter went unto Joppa. When Peter arrived, he kicked everyone out of the room where Tabitha was laying. All of a sudden, Peter bent over and whispered into Tabitha's ear, "Arise." As I was laying in my bed I saw what was like a spirit warm, loving, and calm come quickly over to me and told me to arise, grabbed me by my hand and I felt my spirit being lifted up. I jumped up from my bed.

Finally I went back to sleep and went into a dream the Spirit of the Lord said, "Tabitha look," and when I went to look behind me I saw a cross. The Spirit of the Lord said, "This is what you have to bear-this cross." I cried so hard, when I woke up I was really crying. I knew God was showing me, *me*. God often spoke to me in dreams and showed me visions. This is how I knew that my ex-husband was texting on the phone and was not faithful to the marriage. The Spirit of the Lord showed me and it ended up being exactly what He showed me.

Today God is now uncovering the truth folks are being shown themselves and we need to be swift to listen, slow to speak and slow to wrath. Wait for God to choose the man for you. Currently God has placed me in another Ministry and I believe with all my heart that God chose my husband I have right now (a great man of God) for me. We connected the first day we met and still connect after 18 months. I love him so much. Assistant Pastor Eddie L. Shannon at *Under The Blood House of Prayer A Deliverance Center*. I have learned recently you can't direct all your love to your mate first. God must be first in everything. The Bible says in Matthew 6:33, *"But seek ye first the kingdom of God, and his righteousness; and all these things shall be added unto you."* My love for God goes up then God sends that love down to my husband, and now we are connected! It's like a triangle… the closer I get to Jesus is the better I become as a Christian and wife.

I encourage all women/men to wait on the Lord! Psalm 27:14, *"Wait on the Lord: be of good courage, and he shall strengthen thine heart: wait, I say, on the Lord."* Why do I say wait on the Lord? Because you will find yourself making a choice from your flesh and there are consequences behind the choices we all make!

I live on Romans 8:28, *"And we know that all things work together for good to them that love God, to them who are then called according to his purpose."* The closer you get to Jesus, the more He will direct your path in all areas of this life, and in the second coming of eternal life.

I would like to Praise God for all the people He has placed in my life during my trials, tribulations, and currently I Praise God for my Florida Parent's Bishop Anthony, and Prophetess Yolanda Williams, Pastor Barbara J. Neal, and Gaynell Shannon. I would like to Praise God for My mother in Brooklyn, N.Y., Margaret R Lambert-Porcher, Grandmother, Reverend Isabel Jessamy, Pastor Lloyd and Cynitha Mcleggan, My Prayer Partner, all of my siblings, and family. I love you all so much, and Praise God for your guidance and support. God Bless………..

~Min. Tabitha Shannon

Dear Lord, I Think I Married The Wrong Person

Sherell Edwards

founder of AGC Transport & Services, LLC, a logistics & international trading company and the Christian Women's Leadership Exchange, Inc., a national association created to support women in Christian leadership roles is known for her laser-focused leadership abilities and entrepreneurial skills. She tends to motivate with high energy and a high level of business savvy.

She wields a Class A license as a commercial truck driver, along with a bachelor's and master's degree, while focusing on the growth and development of her companies and business endeavors.

She is gaining global notoriety as the published author of Chronicles of A Broken Spirit, a four volume, non-fiction book series that consist of the surreal journal entries of a woman who encounters the highs and lows of marriage divorce, choosing a career, Christianity, parenthood and self-identity, released in January 2011 (Please go to www.chroniclesofabrokenspirit.webs.com for more information.)

Dear Lord, I Think I Married The Wrong Person

Sherell, a native of Jacksonville, FL is the proud mother of three and "GLAM-Ma" of two.

Contact Information:

The Christian Women's Leadership Exchange, Inc., P.O. Box 41645, Jacksonville, FL 32203. Email: weareGWGA@gmail.com

Dear Lord, I Think I Married The Wrong Person

Broken to be Made Whole

Some memories fade and others last forever. This particular memory remains with me to this very moment. I was a newlywed in my first months of marriage. We, referring to my former husband and I, were in our new apartment, in the bedroom and a dispute around our beliefs in God was somewhere in the context of our verbal exchange. While the exact words of the entire conversation escape me, my final words are still heard like the sound of a train's horn. I said, "This is not going to work." I knew at that very moment that the marriage would not survive. My spouse at that time rebutted my statement and seemed very indifferent to my words. I remember thinking how nonchalant he was about the major gaps in our conversation about belief in Jesus Christ and attending church and after a day or so; I was able to shrug it off and move forward. Unfortunately, the marriage would end 7 ½ years later.

Let's examine how we even got to this point. There I was a recent college graduate, employed, credit worthy, self-sufficient and the mother of one son while having just ended an "on-again, off-again" relationship of four years. God had truly blessed me to overcome some real hurdles, but there I was at the tender age of 23 and had spent the last four years of my life loving someone else who obviously was not ready to actually marry me. Oh, I had received an engagement ring about two years prior that indicated some intent. Yet, my former boyfriend chose to meet other female "friends", not answer his phone at times and a number of other controlling behaviors that would prevent us from getting close to a final commitment.

Dear Lord, I Think I Married The Wrong Person

So, I painfully decided that I had enough going as a young woman to move forward and I could find someone who did want to marry someone like me... and that's just what I did. After all, my former boyfriend and I were not communicating at that time and it was time for me to show him that I could move forward without him.

What started as an emergency incident with my young son and his grandfather out at a restaurant, led me to connect and meet my former husband for the first time. My son's grandfather had taken ill while they were out for breakfast one Saturday morning and apparently the restaurant staff had taken notice of the situation and offered to assist my son with contacting a family member. Naturally, my son gave the store personnel his mother's home phone... MINE!

I happened to be home that morning, although that normally was not the case and answered the phone. There was this distinct, professional male voice on the phone asking for me by name. I hesitated but slowly responded, suspicious of what the call was about. The man on the other end stated he was with my son and went further to explain how my son's grandfather became ill, seemed to be recovering but they wanted to contact a family member to at least notify someone. After securing the location, I agreed to drive over just to make sure everything was okay.

So naturally, like any mother concerned, dressed in sweats, tennis shoes and no frills, I took off for the restaurant. Upon arrival, my son's grandfather and son were seated together and his drop in blood sugar had been resolved. I inquired more seriously, but was soon backed off by the grandfather who proudly, minimized the situation and insisted that things were "fine". Without much fuss, I sat as they continued breakfast and waited to see for myself if things were indeed, "fine." In the meantime, little did I know I was being observed by one of the store manager trainees who sat down on the other end of the seating area. I looked around, seeking patience and eventually our eyes met.

This young male, managing paperwork and seated near other employees looked me dead in my eyes. He did not hesitate to summons me over with a finger motion. I had to grasp and internalize this non-verbal gesture towards me for a few seconds. Finally, I pointed towards myself, in response to the initial fingering gesture and he nodded in affirmation that the gesture was indeed, intended for me. I got up, went over to where this guy was seated and he informed me that he was the person who called the home earlier and explained the situation. He went on to elaborate how mature he thought my son was and wanted to meet the person who was raising such a responsible child. He said he was a management trainee in town for training from two states nearby and wanted to know if he could "keep" my phone number. After some extended verbal exchange, the conversation ended with him "keeping" my number, a date later that night, a long-distance relationship and his relocation and our marriage all within a five month period.

Why such a major decision in such a short period of time? I simply saw the potential with this man as a husband, he was employed in a management position, showed some interest in my son, he was interested in moving to FL and BEST OF ALL- he was

Dear Lord, I Think I Married The Wrong Person

interested in marriage… "*JACKPOT*" I was the one person others loved to underestimate *at least in my mind* so not only had I accomplished a four-year college degree after such a gloomy past, but now, I would add a new husband to my list of achievements and "in your face" moments.

While for me the marriage was a message of success for many to behold, it was also meant to be a flashing moniker for my former boyfriend of four years to let him know I was able to achieve marriage without him and in quite a timely fashion. In other words, it did not take me long to show him that I would have what I wanted (to get married), with or without him. Yes, even back then, I was a determined young woman.

I was aware of God, attended church regularly and knew he had been an integral part of my life, but I did not have a personal relationship with Christ. So you don't have to guess that I certainly was not knowledgeable of His Word or the institution of marriage. It is so amazing though how He used this marriage to bring me to my knees, closer to the Word and even more so, to develop faith and belief in Him.

What I thought would be a message sender (the marriage itself) to all those who knew my past and doubted me ended up being my own personal message and testimony that led to my development of a personal relationship with Jesus Christ. There is absolutely no way I would be here to share my story without Him.

In hindsight, I knew very early on in the marriage that I had made a big mistake yet I remained there for another seven plus years, constantly hoping for survival without all the necessary tools and knowledge not to mention there were children involved. Those factors I considered to be important were suddenly not as important as whether we would serve the same living God and similar religious beliefs. Actually, there was a major conflict with my Methodist background (going to church) and his Jehovah's Witnesses background (attending the Hall), although he was inactive in status.

The cute little annoyances in the relationship that seemed like love at the beginning were not so cute in everyday life. Not only had I married on the rebound, but so had my former spouse. He had been in a relationship that was not going like he wanted and I can only assume the marriage was an opportunity to do something better and different because he would relocate to a new state, with a new job in a big city with new opportunities.

We soon became married but no friendship had developed. I could go on about various different things that were controversial within this union but simply put, *God was not in the presence of this marriage at the start.* Instead of seeking God's guidance for marriage and a mate, I went out and made my own decision and reaped the consequences of such a poorly made decision.

Three years into the marriage I found a bible-believing church that my son and I joined, my son was baptized and I attended without my spouse on a regular basis. This was stressful at times learning so much about the Lord and not being able to happily share the Word with the other adult in my home. This along with feelings of complete loneliness, were the toughest things to deal with within the marriage. In the midst of the union, there I was learning what God intended the institution of marriage to be and how God's Word was the answer key to all the things I was unsure about.

After seven and a half years of marriage, my former spouse decided he no longer loved me and chose to be with someone else. He had started a new relationship through his job and once I found out, I initiated the divorce process. During those seven years, our family had expanded from three members to five, because a set of twins had been born. We were a close knit unit because of the children and the divorce was a very difficult period of adjustment for all three of them. What our three children had known as a complete family was being disrupted and each one of them dealt with it differently. From behavioral outbursts in public settings to withdrawal, our children were torn by the divorce and it took some time for them to regain balance. Not only had I suffered but I opened an opportunity for my children to suffer as well and this was very difficult to endure. This indeed, was the most difficult part of the divorce experience.

Although wounded, hurt and worn, the Lord would not allow me to accept defeat. He put it on my heart to ease the hurt, pain and tragedy my children experienced by creating new, positive memories within our single parent setting. I would plan specific vacation times and family dates that would allow for closeness, bonding and fun with my kids as a single mother. I intentionally set times for family dinners so that eventually those broken hearts would mend and the fragments of our former life would fade. Jesus allowed these times to occur, to heal us all and bring us even closer. The tragedy that once tore us apart ended up being the event that brought us closer than ever.

Dear Lord, I Think I Married The Wrong Person

Family time since has become a part of our family lifestyle and we still operate as a family unit like this to this day. My children have awaken on the grounds of Disney World on Christmas Day, attended NBA games live and on TNT sports television, shopped all day and relaxed in various resorts and suites during vacations. I use those vacation examples not as bragging rights but as a witness to the hand of the Savior and what He does in the lives of his children to restore us. He made opportunities available for our latter days as a single parent family to be greater than times before. Now pardon me as I take a praise break moment here!

God is so awesome that I do not have many detailed memories of the divorce process but I do remember the scripture, I Cor. 7: 12-17 via one of those bible taught, Sunday sermons. It gives specific instruction as to how to conduct ourselves when a wife or husband is married to an unbeliever, even more specifically v. 15. Jesus always gives us an opportunity to repent and to be restored. How did God know so many of us would go down this rugged road and need this type of instruction and reprieve? He truly did allow me to find peace. It was a peace that I had never known before, as I rested in His care.

Eventually, I came to realize that I needed growth in many areas and more specifically in the way I made major decisions and why. I accepted that not everything was black and white and that uncertainty should lead to more examination (I John 4:1) and less anxiety (Phil. 4:6). Now, I invite the Lord in to my decision-making process. I felt like a failure after my divorce and decided that I would never be strong enough, wise enough or experienced enough to make a decision about marriage or anything without taking it in prayer to My Savior.

Alignment with the Lord places me in a winning position and I can already attest to what happens when we operate and make decisions outside of His will. In the same context, I know this marriage was by far no mistake, but a training ground that God used to bring me closer to him and towards my destiny within the Kingdom.

I learned so many important things throughout and beyond the end of the marriage like loving those who have hurt you, forgiveness, soft answers that turn away wrath, being unequally yoked, understanding seasons and God's perfect timing and more. As we can also see, my motives for marriage were not pure. How dare I take God's institution to uplift my own pride and show others up? God was not pleased and He chastises those He loves (Heb. 12:6).

I now respect the institution of marriage and those couples who work daily to make it work. Marriage is far from easy and not something to be taken lightly. I look in admiration at couples that have overcome past infidelity, communication problems, financial stressors, illnesses, distance, and various issues because there are so many successful marriages out here that have overcome tough hurdles.

Now I look at and admire married couples who continue to make it work they give me hope, a picture of success and a renewed spirit that should I marry again, success is more than possible. Forget what the media, statistics and negative attitudes have said; know that God does not foster failure. In the meantime, I cherish my love affair with the Savior and the times I have to just focus on my relationship with Him and self-improvement.

I understand that marriage is honorable but not a requirement to serve Him and that as a single woman my first duty is to stay focused on His will and purpose for my life. Like any other, there are things I would have done differently to yield a better result. I did not seek Christ first prior to my marriage, but allowed my flesh and pride to lead me to pain. I learned the true meaning of Prov. 3:5-6 which discounts leaning upon my own understanding and to acknowledge Him, or His position in my life and He would direct my path. This has become one of my favorite passages of scripture. In the meantime, He has given me much to do and I have chosen to believe it will lead me to my best life ever. I am being content in whatever state I am in (Phil. 4:11) which promotes happiness from within. I know the Lord only wants the best for His children and I am one of His. *Believe without any doubt that blessings are on the way.*

Since the divorce, the Savior has used me to accomplish even more. Although, I am still a single parent, my oldest child is now a 25-year old adult and those twins are teenagers who balance a rigid academic life and quality social life activities. I went from employee to small business owner and now global entrepreneur, leveraging my time between several businesses, one of which includes an association which supports the authorship of my first book, *Chronicles of A Broken Spirit* released January 2011. The association is a form of Christian ministry as it caters to women in Christian leadership roles and was birthed immediately following a 40-day fast (October 2009). Much of my witness attests to the obedience of the Father. I learned that by prayer, fasting and supplication, *that all things,* not some, but *all* are possible when we have unwavering faith. God truly is faithful to those that love and seek after Him.

Let's Recap some things.

- There are no accidents or mistakes in life. God *allows* everything to happen for a reason, even divorce;

- The Word (or Holy Bible) is the guidebook of life. It answers and guides us in all aspects of life;

- That strange feeling in the pit of your stomach is the Holy Spirit, or the helper that Jesus sent to aid us, lead us and guide us. If it feels strange or not right, then heed the warning. The Holy Spirit is there to aid us and many times save us from pain and grief;

- Being a Christian, does not guarantee anyone a stress free and crisis free life. Belief in Christ simply means, we have the support we need to get us through those tough times;

- The institution of marriage should not be taken lightly and requires a sound foundation in order to last. It is not a seasonal act but a long-term commitment that comes with real challenges;

- Poor decision-making can often affect others (family, children, etc.) as well as ourselves. Invite Christ into your decision-making process and be patient in receiving His answer;

- Tragedies are not final. Prayer and faith in the Lord can move us to victory. The Savior hears our prayers and is faithful even when we are not;

- ❖ Every decision does not call for a "black and white" resolution. When there are things we are uncertain of, the Word tells us what to do in I John 4:1. The Lord also, advises us what we should avoid in Phil. 4:6

- ❖ Heed the Lord's guidance through the Holy Spirit. Make sure that your goals are in alignment with the Lord's will for your life. That's the only true way to success;

- ❖ Develop a healthy view of marriage and seek positive examples of it through couples you know personally and socially. Remember, that marriage is the Lord's institution and He does not foster failure;

- ❖ Learn, read and refer to Prov. 3:5-6

- ❖ God loves His children and only wants the best for us. Seek Him for your best and He will honor your prayers.

I offer the following advice for those, who feel you want to be married, re-married and need that daily companionship, go to God and make sure you are ready. Many times, we are anxious for the next step but God has not granted our heart's desire because we have not done the work to position ourselves to receive His blessing(s).

Loved ones, let's do the work. Let's forgive our past transgressors not for them but for us; let's be a real friend, so we know how to identify and operate as one; let's be happy for others when their turn in line has arrived; let's be selfless with service because its' only when we sow "BIG", that we reap "BIG".

Dear Lord, I Think I Married The Wrong Person

In the Bible, Ruth was diligently working the fields of Boaz when he found her. Notice, she was busy about her work, when she was found; Ruth was not on the chat line, phone lines and in the bar rooms seeking for herself. When we take care of God's business, then he loves to take care of ours. Ruth went from working the fields to being the wife of the owner of those fields. The Lord blesses like that!

If you have not done anything for someone else that does not benefit you, then it is highly likely you are not ready for marriage. There is plenty of sacrifice and work involved. Let's work on ourselves, understand our roles and do what we were meant to do well. Before you know it, God's blessing will have found you and will be more than your mind can imagine. Wait on His answer no matter how long it takes because I am sure it will be better than any best laid plan we can come up with!

The Lord is faithful to all His promises and loving toward all He has made. ~Psalm 145:13

~ Sherell Edwards

Dear Lord, I Think I Married The Wrong Person

DaNita L. Greene

currently resides in the Southern Region of New Jersey and works as an Office Manager for a non-profit organization. She is the mother of an adult daughter whom she adores.

DaNita received her certification as a Professional Development Coach & Energy Leadership Index Master Practitioner from the Institute for Professional Excellence in Coaching (iPEC); and also has a certification in Women's Issues & Diversity Training from the Professional Woman's Network where she also holds membership. To date she has co-authored two books and is presently working on her next literary project. *"The Power Of God"* is the first installment in a series of Christian books & daily devotionals that will be published by Christmas 2012.

DaNita is a member of *True Servant Worship & Praise Church* in Hamilton, New Jersey, where Bishop E.E. Jenkins is Senior Pastor. She serves on the council of the *HEELS Women's Ministry*, which stands for **H**elping, **E**ncouraging, **E**steeming & **L**ifting **S**isters.

Dear Lord, I Think I Married The Wrong Person

One of her greatest missions is to bring to fruition the ministry & business GOD placed on the inside of her, to Empower, Motivate & Inspire women from the inside-out.

For inquiries, you may contact DaNita
via e-mail at www.destinyseekers22@gmail.com
and she can also be found on Facebook & followed on Twitter.

*A special thanks to TLD Consulting Enterprise

Dear Lord, I Think I Married The Wrong Person

Looking For Love In All The Wrong Places

Instead Of Seeking The Love Within

When I was 11 yrs. old I was sexually violated by a trusted foe. It was at that time seeds of hurt, shame, fear, distrust, worthlessness and unworthiness were planted. I quickly learned how to suppress my feelings and move on. How many of you know you will never conquer what you won't/don't confront?! Unbeknownst to me this would have a major impact on my life for many years in relation to my interactions with men. I began looking outside of myself to fill a void that I thought had been taken away or lost. The enemy had set a trap, but GOD had a plan… **Love.**

I was introduced to my ex-husband by a mutual friend. We were instantly attracted to one another and quickly fell in love. I had waited so long for the right man to come along, one whom I wanted to marry and who wanted to marry me. I believed GOD had finally sent me a husband. I was so in love and so happy. He knew I was saved and it was okay that he wasn't because GOD was going to use me to draw him into The Kingdom. After all, I knew plenty of Christians who married unsaved mates, fornicated and a whole lot of other stuff and they seemed to be doing just fine. The Word said that the unbelieving husband would be sanctified by the believing wife. (I Corinthians 7:14). *How many of you know there's a price to pay for disobedience unto GOD?!*

Dear Lord, I Think I Married The Wrong Person

We lived a distance from one another so early on as our friendship was being established we communicated a lot over the phone and through letters. It was all good… at first. We had our little disagreements, nothing too serious but I later realized they were really warning signs. I was walking into this situation with my "eyes wide shut." We both brought our own issues into this union. I needed to be complete and my husband was going to make it happen, he needed to get on his feet and I was going to make that happen. He had issues with his mother which eventually manifested into disrespect towards me. I was going to love that right out of him because love conquers all. We were going to make this marriage work with our damaged selves. *How many of you know that before you can love anyone else, you must first love GOD, yourself and also be able to receive* it?!

There were many, many warning signs. First from the start we were unequally yoked in our GODLY beliefs or the lack thereof. We married the evening before our scheduled wedding date because there was a huge snowstorm expected. So, what was supposed to have been our wedding rehearsal ended up being our actual wedding ceremony. Earlier that week we had one of our famous arguments and weren't even speaking when we got married. Our vows were the first words we spoke to one another that day. *How many of you know GOD is always speaking to His sons and daughters but we're not always listening?!*

As you can see the relationship started off rocky and it only got worse. Every time it seemed as if things were getting better something would happen and it would get even worse. When it was good it was very good but when it was bad it was horrible. The more I showed him love the more irritated he

Dear Lord, I Think I Married The Wrong Person

became with me and total rejection would be the final outcome. I would be so hurt because I truly loved him and really wanted my marriage to work. I wanted him to feel the love that he said he never received and the best way to do it was to continue to pray and study to make sure what I was doing as a wife lined-up with the Word of GOD.

But he would misunderstand and/or resist practically everything I would do for him. I later realized that I was looking for something from him that he wasn't able to give and the result would be verbal, mental and sometimes physical abuse. Then I would just shut down because I couldn't understand why I would do something good and be rewarded in such a cruel way. When he did nice things for me I would show my heartfelt appreciation. I began to believe GOD had turned away from me, and why would HE do that? I must have been doing something wrong but I didn't know what so I kept praying. *How many of you know that GOD will never leave you nor forsake you?!~* Hebrews 13:5

Birthdays and holidays were big in our house and it was his birthday so I planned a surprise dinner for him at a really nice restaurant in Philadelphia, Pa. I had created theatre tickets to make it seem like we were going to a play. The dining room table was decorated with balloons and a beautiful cake. I invited friends & family but his friends who lived a distance weren't able to come. Well we almost didn't make it because he tried to start this big argument over nothing. He knew I had made plans for his birthday, he just didn't know exactly what the plans were. Well I ended up having to tell him and he went grudgingly. But once we got there with everyone, he was a different person, thank GOD.

Dear Lord, I Think I Married The Wrong Person

This would be the way he acted most of the time, and then when we were in the company of others he would turn back into the man I first met and fell in love with. He later told me he acted this way because he wasn't use to anyone treating him so good. My thought was okay *I understand, but it's still unacceptable!* I would continue to ask GOD why?

If you were on the outside looking in you would have thought we had it going on! Nice big house, nice cars, clothes, jewelry, money in the bank and bills paid. I had a beautiful wedding ring and it would just sparkle. I remember I use to say to GOD that I wanted my marriage to sparkle & shine just like my wedding ring. *How many of you know GOD wants us to prosper in every area of our lives?! Behold, I pray that you may prosper in all things, and be in health, just as your soul prospers.* ~3 John 2

I always paid my tithes and he'd learned enough about tithing to know somebody needed to pay them. But he wasn't interested in paying his own tithes or us paying our tithes as a couple. We both worked hard to build and maintain the lifestyle we'd created together. Although he made it clear that his job was more important than mine because he worked harder and made more money than I did. The material things most couples desired, we had it. *How many of you know "seek ye first the kingdom of GOD and His righteousness; and all these things shall be added unto you!* ~ Matthew 6:33

He came home every evening to a clean house and a home cooked meal. No matter how he treated me or what happened between us I never refused him physical intimacy. This was not always easy but HE never said it would be easy. I did it because I

Dear Lord, I Think I Married The Wrong Person

knew GOD would honor His Word and my obedience. *"Let the husband render to his wife the affection due her, and likewise also the wife to her husband. The wife does not have authority over her own body, but the husband does. And likewise the husband does not have authority over his own body, but the wife does."* ~ 1 Corinthians 7:3-4

Many times things wouldn't go the way he planned and he would blame me for it. We bought a home in a location that he chose that was a total of 3 hours driving time per day to and from his job. There was a storm one evening and on his way home from work he got into an accident. No one got hurt thank GOD. When he arrived I got cursed out and blamed for it because if he wasn't married to me he would have stayed where he was instead of jeopardizing his life to get home to me. He knew if he had called to say he was staying because of the storm it wouldn't have been any problem.

I loved my ex-husband and loved being a wife but the "otherness" which is what I called the mental, verbal and physical abuse, became harder and harder for me to deal with. Let me just say we both grew up in New Jersey, he was from Newark and I was from Trenton. I had been pushed over, looked over and put down long enough, so you weren't just going to say anything to me or treat me any kind of way.

The more I would hear him refer to me as the 'B' word or I hate marriage or I wish I never married you, which was often, I would no longer be hurt, just angry. I would then go straight up flesh on him, "Who do you think you're talking to?" and "You better watch how you treat me, I AM a child of the living King," and "I don't want nobody that don't want me and furthermore, who put a gun to your head, we did not have a shot-gun wedding!" *How many of you know this only made matters worse because "we do not wrestle against flesh and blood, but against principalities, against powers, against the rulers of the darkness of this age, against spiritual hosts of wickedness in heavenly places* ~Ephesians 6:12

He began hanging out more and more, sometimes he would come home and sometimes he would not. He came home one night and told me that there was someone trying to take him away from me and to be honest at that time I was ready for him to go. He said that he still loved me but he was no longer in love with me I immediately recognized whose words were being spoken out of his mouth because although he may have felt that way he would never talk that way. *How many of you know that no one can take another from you they willingly go?!*

I knew what time it was but I also knew I was not going to leave him I had made a covenant unto GOD and I was not about to break it. The truth of the matter is if he had continued to stay at home I would still be there doing whatever it took to save my marriage. *How many of you know GOD had a plan?!*

He finally left, GOD allowed it and I didn't have the desire nor need to go after him. I did what I'd done throughout my entire marriage which was pray and seek scripture to stand on. *How many of you know "ask, and it shall be given you, seek and you shall find, knock and it shall be opened unto you* ~ Matthew 7:7 The Holy Spirit divinely directed me to a scripture that gave me the peace that surpassed all my understanding and the liberty to weather the storm of divorce. *But if the unbeliever departs, let him*

Dear Lord, I Think I Married The Wrong Person

depart, a brother or a sister is not under bondage in such cases. But GOD has called us to peace." ~ 1 Corinthians 7:15

We were married in the year 2000, separated in 2006 and divorced in 2009. I later found out that at the time of our divorce his mistress was pregnant and afterwards they married and had a healthy baby girl. I wish them all the best which is Salvation through our Lord and Savior, JESUS Christ!

I now know that during my wilderness experience in my marriage, I too was pregnant and all the hurt I'd experienced was just labor pains. GOD was busy filling that void that I believed had left me when I was sexually violated at 11 yrs. old. He said I was created whole & complete and I AM fearfully and wonderfully made. He has brought such clarity to questions I'd had concerning my marriage and my life. GOD had impregnated me with a ministry that was down on the inside of me, and gifts & talents I never knew existed in me. He has birthed out of me a Kingdom Builder, on fire for GOD. In a million years I would have never believed my life would be on this path that GOD has set before me. I AM Thankful & Grateful Unto GOD and Live Each Day Now In Great Expectation About My Future!

Dear Lord, I Think I Married The Wrong Person

My Encouragement To You

- ❖ Know That The Greatest Love Of All Dwells On The Inside Of You, Seek It & Cultivate It!

- ❖ You Are Fearfully & Wonderfully Made!

- ❖ In All Things Seek GOD, Your Pain Is Not In Vain!

- ❖ Know That GOD Is Speaking Even When You Don't Hear Him!

- ❖ No Matter What Is Going On In Your Life or The Lives Of Others, Be Obedient To What GOD Is Instructing You To Do!

- ❖ Your Test Will Become Your Testimony!

- ❖ GOD Is Working Behind The Scenes For You Even When You Can't See It!

- ❖ To All The Caterpillars, The Metamorphosis Is Almost Over, Be Encouraged, You're About To Emerge As A Butterfly!

- ❖ GOD Always Sends Warnings Before The Fall- Pay Attention!

- ❖ What GOD Has For You, It Is For You!

- ❖ Never Look For Someone Else To Complete You – GOD Already Created You Whole!

Dear Lord, I Think I Married The Wrong Person

- ❖ Everybody's Journey Is Different, Focus on the Path GOD Has Set Before You!

- ❖ You Have To First Love GOD & Yourself Before You Can Love Anyone Else!

- ❖ GOD Will Turn Your Mess Into A Message – Be Patient

*~**<u>For your Maker is your husband</u>**, The Lord of hosts is His name; And your Redeemer is the Holy One of Israel; He is called the God of the whole earth.~* Isaiah 54:5 (NKJV)

~DaNita L. Greene

Dear Lord, I Think I Married The Wrong Person

Evangelist Genita Gentry

Was born and raised in Cincinnati, Ohio. In 1996 she joined the United States Navy and relocated to Virginia Beach, Virginia where she still current resides along with her two daughters, Kyaunna and Khadiya.

Her testimony is *You can overcome if you tap into your God given purpose and walk in it!* Because of this she is very passionate about people and helping others. She gives much of her time to various charities and to those in need.

She is the Author of "*Embracing the Inner You*" a book that defines the trials of being exposed to drugs, alcoholism and even at one point being homeless at a very young age.

Evangelist Gentry has had the opportunity to travel around the United States as well as other countries Evangelizing and Preaching the Gospel. She has two more books coming out this summer and a Gospel Jazz album due out Winter 2012. Be on the look-out for what God is doing in this young Evangelist life!

Her testimony of life's challenges say ~ *In all you do ensure that God gets the Glory!*

You may contact Genita at dvynemin@gmail .

Dear Lord, I Think I Married The Wrong Person

Dear Lord, A Puzzle is Not Complete Without You

In 1998 I moved to Norfolk, Virginia to check onboard my very first ship. At the time I had been in the Navy for almost 2 years. My daughter's father had walked out of me and my daughter's life but my two year old little girl made my life worth living. All I was missing was the perfect husband and I could only pray that he would eventually find me.

Although I was a single parent and at the time had no place to live, I was excited about my new job. My grandmother was taking care of my daughter in Cincinnati while I got stable, found child care, transportation and somewhere to call home. As the new girl on the ship I found a new friendship with a co-worker, he wasn't the finest thing walking onboard the ship but he dressed real nice, was funny, sweet, and sincere and he made me forget about all my real life problems when I was around him. He had a vehicle so he gave me a good excuse to get off the ship and get some air during the week. At first I just viewed him as a close friend we would often go out to eat, out to the movies, etc. I was 2 years older than him. He was charming and often attracted much older women.

On any given day some dude on the ship would try to take me out on a date. They would use my coworkers to get my attention and one day they gave "him" a message, *why did they do that?* At the time I did not see anything wrong with exchanging numbers and meeting them, "so I said sure, give him my number," truly bad idea. Next thing I know all I heard was "What is the world is wrong with you? I don't want you to care about any of these other dudes all I want is you." OMG! I was beyond surprised I had no idea he felt this way, honestly I really cared for him but just not in that way, I truly had some thinking to do because at the time I saw him as baggage and I wasn't ready for someone who had a baby on the way plus a son that he had as a teenager, and not to mention quite a few of older mature women after him.

After a couple days of thinking I told him yes we can try to make a relationship work but first he needed to change his number and drop all those other women. I wasn't having it, *those chicks got to go*! I wonder how many hearts do you think he broke just to win mine?

Well it's been 6 months of bliss and happiness of course every relationship has problems but through it all, I loved this man. In my mind this man completed me- we struggled a little with our finances we loved to shop till we dropped. We both honestly believed we were still saved and loved God but at the time our hearts were far from serving Him.

So that is why we decided to shack up before marriage, truly a bad idea, but it seemed like a good idea at the time. Also I should add my boyfriend is a preacher's kid. Not really understanding that if we truly were sincere about our relationship Christ needed to be the center. We both grew up in church and sang in the church choir but you could tell by our lifestyle that Christ wasn't the center.

Dear Lord, I Think I Married The Wrong Person

Truthfully our relationship was a tad materialistic, true love can never be founded on material things, the car he or she drives, how he dresses but yes that was really big in our relationship. One day while at the mall marriage came up and he just said "Let's get married." I looked at him for a second and couldn't help to think *well we already living like we are married, the ring is the only thing missing*, so I said, "Yes".

We did the typical military shotgun marriage; invite two close friends as witnesses and on February 14, of 2000 we on our way to martial bliss. Being married made me feel so complete with my daughter and now a husband and a cute little apartment. The worst thing a person can do is marry to complete a puzzle before truly knowing who they are with the Creator. I raise my hand on this one that was me!

June of 2000 was the day that I dreaded, my husband was going on a six month deployment. When that ship left that pier I cried so badly you would have thought that man provided oxygen to me. While my husband was away I had to reinvent myself with finding things to do around the house, going to back to school, spending time with my daughter, social gatherings and making new friends. At my new job I got really close with someone who was from my hometown who became really like a big sister to me. She always had something positive to say often talking about God, just a really genuine friendly mature woman.

Finally in December of 2000 and the schedule was revised by a few days my husband was finally coming home! I was the happiest woman ever when that man got off the ship, he's a rather big guy and had been in the gym during the whole deployment so when he walked off he had trimmed up and was looking like a quarterback. We spent time together and I did not want to let him out of my sight.

Not sure what happened over the course of three month but all of a sudden things started to shift, family weekends turned into night out with the boys and when I would call to see when he would be home I would often get voicemail and a return call saying he lost track of time. Mind you he is leaving at noon returning home around 8 or 9pm every Saturday night.

Now it has been four months since my husband has been back and we have now graduated from newlywed status with our first anniversary. We had also graduated from occasional arguing to fighting and fussing just about every weekend. I quickly noticed that not one of my husband's friends was married, they were all single. Married people should not hang out with single people that do a whole bunch single people things. It has become routine for me to call asking when he was coming home.

One day I had a vivid dream which till this day I considered prophetic. I dreamt that I caught my husband cheating on me with the same woman, for one week I dreamt the same dream with the same girl. These dreams got so intense one day I woke up like it was real, turned over, hit my husband and called him a name that I will not repeat. I guess things were finally starting to add up but was I ready to receive what God was revealing to me? Was my heart prepared for the outcome?

In April of 2001 we decided to go over my babysitter's house for a barbeque and some family time. There was a family friend of theirs over there, let's just say she was single and ready to mingle. The whole time we were there she did not even try to hide her advances towards my husband and I did not like my husband's responses. Thank God I remained classy the whole night. But when we got home that night, I went totally belligerent on my husband and yes this did not go over too well with him because he returned the favor.

We argued so much that night next thing you know we were fighting physically, one trip to the emergency room then back home, needless to say my husband ended up serving couch duty that night. The next day he went to work and called home apologizing I asked him what time he was coming home, he simply replied, "I think I am going to sleep on the ship today." I was so hurt when he said that I just wanted him to come home.

Many days passed we both felt guilty about a lot of things and in the end he thought it was best if he stayed away from home. Well remember the mature friend, we are now more like big sister, little sister and I would often find myself calling her for advice. **Let me tell you in the times of trouble control you just got to keep your emotions in check and pray.** The bible says pray without ceasing, I found myself doing what you call back-slider knee ministry. She told me to pray and ask God to heal and restore my marriage. Now that I am wiser I know to pray the prayer of God's will for my life.

A month goes by of separation, tears, hurts and pain. I found out through word of mouth that he was playing basketball every Wednesday so I decided to take my daughter and go to the gym to see if we could talk. As I was about to walk in the

Dear Lord, I Think I Married The Wrong Person

building my husband comes in the parking lot and as he got out of the car you would have thought I was mud or gum on the ground he didn't even acknowledge me or my daughter, then on the passenger side someone gets out the car and to my dismay it was a female.

All I could think back to was my dream in March. You have to love yourself enough in some situations to just walk away and remain in character. After seeing this woman and humbling myself in my responses I was beyond stressed sometimes going days without eating, sleeping or going anywhere accept work. I found myself getting back into church, not truly understanding where I went wrong.

To me praying was doing the total opposite of what "I" desired. It was so strange the more I prayed for God to fix it the further me and my husband remained. We became so distant even to the point we started to only communicate through email usually with a blank void questionable emails stating *he still loved me but needed some room*.

It was now a question of do I hold on or let go. I often heard that *real love is worth fighting for*, let me tell you, that we will be fighting spiritual battles all our life especially if you are walking in purpose but if you find yourself fighting physically, pack your bags and then ask God to *order your steps* like the Word of God says.

After three months of separation this so called love resulted in me fighting his mistress in public and going to court fighting over a man who actions towards me did not display love.

Dear Lord, I Think I Married The Wrong Person

Was this love worth all this, serving one day in jail with eighty-nine days suspended, one year probation, one hundred hours of community service plus court fees and fines, *NO!* and it was definitely my wake up call.

No one should ever have to fight a physical fight to keep their spouse. I realized that I wasn't the perfect wife and my ex-husband truly wasn't a bad person he just made bad choices and I could be demanding at times and little self-centered often saying, "It's my world I am just letting you live in it". *Thank you God for the change that you now rest in me!*

Lessons Learned

I had to learn never look to someone to complete you; you should meet them already complete; if God be in the union you represent oneness with the creator, creating perfect harmony within the relationship.

My marriage was fulfilling the void of being a single parent with no husband, filling the void of going to bed every night alone. There was a sense of security in being in a relationship, sometimes being by myself made me fill incomplete as if I wasn't a whole person and this is something I should have given over to God *before* getting married. Right now in my personal walk with Christ and especially as an Evangelist for the Gospel I know that the void that I was trying to fill only God could have filled it and made me whole.

If I would have gotten back to my first love (Jesus) those voids would have been filled with the love that God gives us when we totally walk in obedience with Him and for Him. There are so many people who marry for the wrong reasons and don't make God the center; it is through God that the covenant of marriage is created. Not truly understanding that God never intended for me to get married to my ex but, it was truly a life lesson for me and I am sure many have shared similar experiences.

In every marriage I can't stress this enough, Call on Jesus and pray, don't call your mother, father or some psychic psycho for answers. You truly have to yield not to your own understanding and give your entire marriage to God. The worst thing I did was allow other people's opinions to affect my responses and outcomes, never let anyone tell you to leave and get a divorce, God is the only one who can tell you what your next step is, *any situation.*

Understand if you do not have a relationship with your first love, only expect to have carnal, fleshly, worldly driven relationships. Some will not even involve love they will be that evil first cousin often mistaken for love called *lust.*

I am now born again, complete in Jesus Christ, I know who I am and who's I am. Because I know who I belong to now I know that I married to the wrong person for all the wrong reasons. ***For everything I have been through my biggest accomplishment amongst being born again was forgiving and moving forward.*** After the decision was made to move forward I tried to continue to fill the loneliness void only realizing that hurt people, hurt people. I dated just for the reason to make someone feel the way I did often leading men on to only leave them thinking I cared for them. I was still so in love with my husband.

Take some time out to heal. *You must be free from your past in order to prepare for the future.* Single people must operate in obedience to God's word. Yes, that means no fornication or shacking up; you have got to learn how to wait! Don't block or delay your blessings by moving out of God's will. God knew every mistake, trial and tribulation that I was going to make and everything made me stronger. He never left me, I left Him.

Dear Lord, I Think I Married The Wrong Person

There is a man that God will specifically hand-pick for me that will be the priest of our home, my lover, keeper, prayer warrior, my spiritual covering, best friend, he will love me like Christ's first love- the Church.

~Evangelist Genita Gentry

Dear Lord, I Think I Married The Wrong Person

Kendell Lenice

This natural born writer has always had the love of writing and helping people. From the time she was a small child, she has always done both. As a writer, she would write songs, poems, greeting cards, letters, essays, reports…etc, just for the love of it. Writing has always been a part of her everyday life, as well as uplifting others. Kendell always has a positive, inspiring, encouraging word to help those who cross her path. It's just a part of who she is. Both writing and helping others are her passions and what she believes she was put on this earth to do.

Reared in Southern New Jersey, she continued to develop her skills as a writer and participated in many writing competitions in the state. She wrote for local newspapers, school events, weddings, ceremonies…you name it; she would be called to write it. She even won writing scholarships to enter college, as well as to partially cover her tuition.

Kendell Lenice loves to help and encourage others. She believes everyone has a light and everyone's deserves to shine it brightly and boldly. Anyone who knows her knows that is truly important to her. That's how she gets her joy and fulfillment. She wants everyone to know their self-worth and value.

Kendell Lenice resides in Maryland with her two teenage daughters. She continues to pursue her writing career. Her first

Dear Lord, I Think I Married The Wrong Person

novel was Self-published in 2006, entitled, *'Lifetime Membership-No Expiration'*. She has completed her second novel and is looking forward to publishing that in the near future. She has also giving birth to her company, BROWNSTARR (www.brownstarr.com), which she hand makes hair bands/ties for locs, braids, natural hair, thick hair..Etc.) That is her first venture under Brownstarr and she looks to expand that with accessories and much more. Up next "Brownstarr Butta" (shea butter w/natural fragrances) - Available Now. Please stay tuned to, (www. brownstarr.com) there is more to come.

Keep your eyes and ears open for this "Phoenix", you'll never know what she'll do next. Remember her name, Kendell Lenice; you may see her on The New York's Best Seller List and/or in Black Enterprise Magazine, God willing!

"You are a STARR, so don't let anyone dim your shine."

You can contact Kendell by:

Email: kendelllenice@hotmail.com

Website: www.brownstarr.com

Twitter: @klenice

Dear Lord, I Think I Married The Wrong Person

Happily Never After

Marriage Is Not Always a Fairytale

"Once upon a time", "Happily ever after ", "For better or worse", "We are destined" along with other phrases lead us down the road of a fantasies which isn't always good when it comes to marriage.

A wedding is something that many girls/women, aspire to have. Sadly, most girls don't aspire to have a solid marriage. Therefore, the decision to get married is based on theory, infatuation or "perfect timing" more often than most would like to admit. Now some people base their marriage or their prelude to marriage on love or what they perceive to be love but you can't possibly love anyone unless you truly know and love yourself.

A marriage will never work if either the man or woman isn't sure what marriage really is. It is a true commitment to one another and should not have an "easy out clause" if the true commitment is meant to be. However, none of that even matters if God isn't a part of any union. If God isn't the force that drives you individually, then a marriage will never work. If either the man or woman does not believe in God, then run away as fast as you can! If a man or woman says they believe in God, but you never hear them give thanks or make any reverence to the Lord, then run as fast as you can! If God isn't in the forefront of your relationship, then that relationship will fail slowly or drag out to a bitter divorce. Ultimately the relationship will end.

There is no doubt about it. Both individuals have to have the same dedication to God as well as to their relationship. If a man or woman won't pray with you or have a conversation with you about God for whatever reason, then that is a red flag. That is a clear sign that there is some sort of problem.

Putting on your "private eye detective hat" is a must when marrying someone. You have to know what type of relationship they have with their families and friends. That is a must!! A man or woman's relationship with their parents is very important to know. It helps you understand the person better and may prevent you from marrying the person in the first place.

I believe you have to witness the person in their environment and see how they act or react to certain situations. I've said and I've heard people say, "We have a great relationship, we never argue or disagree." That may sound good; however it is not a good thing. Since you are two different people disagreements are inevitable and you need to know before getting married how that person handles conflicts and conflict resolution.

Of course I am not suggesting you pick an argument but I am suggesting you do not commit your life to someone who you have never seen angry or upset with you and seen how they handle those emotions. Often times, couples don't argue "in love." They argue to win or to hurt their spouse, which of course is not love; that marriage is doomed and heading for divorce or you will live miserably until you divorce.

Fortunately and unfortunately, I have been married more than once. The first time I married, I was extremely young. That was more than 20 years ago. (He actually remains one of my very best friends until this day.) I don't regret my learning experiences through my marriages. As I stated, I've learned. I've learned about myself as well as the institution of marriage.

"I think I married the wrong person" There is little to no doubt in my mind. I even had wavering thoughts back then, but I told myself it wasn't that it was the wrong person, but just things I didn't necessarily like. I rationalized my inner thoughts. "Hey no one is perfect, not even I." I try to see the good in everyone and I make excuses at times. This was something that I learned about myself.

My first marriage had already ended in divorce and who is trying to go down that divorce road again? Although that's just where we were headed even before the actual marriage. God was nowhere in our relationship, as far as prayer. He knew the Lord and so did I, but we never prayed together or visited any religious institution or functions together. We never worshiped together in any way, ever. I'd requested and asked, but it wasn't honored. I knew at that point that we were on a slippery slope to divorce. Looking back now, it was never meant to work. It was bound to be an epic fail if we stayed that way. Well, we stayed that way and we are now divorced. Small issues turned into larger issues. If God isn't present in your marriage, then it will not last, bottom line!

The Beginning: I was single and ran into an old friend. The old friend told me he knew the perfect guy for me and wanted to set me up on a blind date. The friend was telling my now ex, the same thing. After weeks of us both declining a blind date, we eventually said "Yes" to the date. That was after my

Dear Lord, I Think I Married The Wrong Person

"ex" asked the friend, "Who is this lady you speak so highly of?" The friend mentioned my name and he said he knew me from years back. The friend didn't believe he knew me, so they called me and it was confirmed. In fact, we did know each other. It was on from there.

He asked me out that same week. We went out on that Thursday, then that Saturday, and continued dating consistently. We soon discovered that we had been acquainted with each other for well over ten years. We use to work together 13 years ago and had been "work friends" and from what I could remember from that time was he was cool, a good guy, a family guy and a funny guy. We were on the fast track and our relationship was moving full speed ahead. At that point our relationship switched from my work friend into, "the man I was dating. We had never been friends outside of work. It had been thirteen years since we had worked together and truthfully, I didn't know him at all. He was nothing like I remembered.

We said we knew one another because of the length of time, but that wasn't really the case. He would always say. "I can't believe I am with Kendell" Now that I look back, that was odd to say. I am far from a celebrity but in a strange way that's how it felt. He would call me by my first and last name. It was almost like he conquered me, in a sense. Now that I think about it. Was that love? He says it was. Hmm… looking back, it makes me wonder.

I always felt that he held me to a very high standard and never left room for me to have flaws. It was hard to be how he thought I should be. He thought I could do no wrong and as a woman. It was very difficult to be perfect 24/7, or even try to be. It was hard to be who he wanted me to be. The "her" he probably wanted at the time was not me. I felt nothing was ever good enough.

Almost right away, we'd talked about marriage, and the importance. We had hopes, dreams and desires that seemed similar, if not the same. We were both divorced and never wanted to go through divorce again. We would be different. We would work because our whole relationship was destiny and fate. That was our thought. *God was not in it so why did we think that?* Prior to that relationship/marriage, I was going to church and learning more about religion. He had a very religious background in the past. He had told me of how the church let him down in a sense.

This was it, we were in love and a future was in our sight. We were planning a life together. "Our love was meant to be", we would always say, to whoever would listen. We focused on how we got together. We told everyone our "love story" and everyone agreed that it was "destiny ," My ex and I were meant to be and live happily ever after. He proposed and I said yes. I truly loved him or what I knew to be love back then. We were excited about our future and our lives together. You couldn't tell us early on that we weren't in love and it wouldn't last.

After a while... I remember having conversations and disagreements which gave us inklings that we should possibly wait on the marriage, but we went full steam ahead. Instead of taking heed to some possible signs, we planned for a wedding (not a marriage). Something didn't seem right, but excuses were made and we proceeded to plan our wedding together. The signs were there to possibly wait as I reflect now, but we didn't. I recall when I was about to walk down the aisle, I was at the top of the aisle ready to walk down, but my feet wouldn't move.

My father asked jokingly, was I sure I wanted to do this. He asked me that because my feet seemed stuck to the floor and I looked dazed. I told my father I was ready and I proceeded to walk down the aisle. We said our vows in front of family and friends, as they smiled at us in joy. However, I'm not sure if it was really deep joy for me. I say because when it was instructed to "kiss your bride." It didn't play out like the fantasy weddings that I've witnessed on television. It played out a little differently.

You know how everyone looks forward to that part of the ceremony. Well, I was probably the only one who was not looking forward to that part of the ceremony. What woman doesn't look forward to kissing the man of her dreams, especially a romantic sap like me? Let me tell you what I did when it was time to "kiss the bride" My husband went to kiss me and I turned my face away from the guests, towards the preacher and "pecked" my husband so no one would see us kiss.

Who does that? Me! I "does" that. That should have told me and the rest of my guests and new husband that something was wrong. I wonder if any of my guests thought that was different? I was told later that a few guests thought he wasn't the "one" for me, but of course they didn't want to say anything. (They did years later.) I truly believe my husband felt some kind of way about that because he just kind of looked at me. I can be shy sometimes, so maybe he thought that. Maybe it was just that at the time.

Dear Lord, I Think I Married The Wrong Person

Don't get me wrong I married him because I thought I loved him, but now I know that it couldn't have been the real deal love. I would not marry anyone if I thought I didn't love him, but later I see it wasn't love. We weren't walking with God together. There was no prayer together in our household. I prayed all the time individually and always have. I'm sure he had done the same, but not together. I would ask if we could together, but we never did. Looking back, that was the official problem in our marriage. Through our short marriage my husband used to always say he thought I didn't love him and I would always say, "Yes I do," and I thought I truly did. As I look back, I really didn't and he was right. He could tell even when I couldn't or didn't want to admit.

I'm not here to air his dirty laundry and say he said or did this or that. Through all relationships there are issues and everyone brings some kind of baggage, no matter how small or large. He's a good person; we just didn't work for a few reasons. It didn't work, it wasn't meant to work. There were several issues that didn't make it a great marriage and the main thing was that God wasn't present in our marriage at all and we married possibly for the wrong reasons.

Our marriage never even made it to the two year mark or should I say we separated a little shy of two years. (We had had some major (tragic) hits to our marriage in such short time that some people don't experience in ten years, so that didn't help. It hurt us. We had no foundation to stay on or refer back to.) Although he says we both ended it. He is the one that filed the papers. I was stuck on the "I don't want to go through a divorce train." "I don't want to be a failure in this." "Let's make it work, even if it's wrong." I came up with so many reasons internally why I shouldn't give up on the marriage. Now I see, staying in the marriage had nothing to do with him. It was all me. I didn't want to stay in the marriage because I loved him so, now I see I just didn't want to divorce or disregard our "family life" together. We had built a family unit. I worried about what others would say... etc, etc.

It was very difficult to go through a divorce when you didn't plan on it. I don't think anyone gets married to get divorced. I believe you truly hope for the best and pray that it will last. Although I knew in my heart early on that it would not last, I was willing to just stay in the marriage. I think I convinced myself that it was truly love. Now I know it was the bliss in the beginning as everyone experiences, but it was not long lasting love. That's the kind of love that's needed.

Could it have worked? Possibly for longer than it did. To last a life time, no. We didn't have what it took to make it last. It was the wrong person. I also know that the respect level wasn't where it needed to be. If you truly love someone then respect will automatically show. I won't speak for him and his flaws, but I know I didn't always speak to him the way a loving wife should speak. Why? Now I see it was because that "Godly love" was not there. I only can be responsible for me and what I do or did. When it's that "right" person I believe the relationship flows differently. It's not forced. Your walk is different. The love is different. It's natural, free flowing.

I truly believe God lead me to that relationship to learn about myself, relationships, and love. I also strongly believe God lead me out of this relationship once I learned what I needed to learn. I now know that this relationship was never meant to last. I also know that God lead me to that relationship to learn and go, not to marry and stay. If I'd married the right person, then I'd still be married. Right?

It was embarrassing and disappointing that I had to go through a divorce. I was very hard on myself. I believe in the institution of marriage, and really wanted to honor my vows. It had less to do with the person, than it had to do with the commitment, which is not right. I know that to be true. I've also learned to listen to the little voice in my head that always leads me down the right road. I've learned not to ignore my inner thoughts. I like to think that God is talking to me. A huge lesson is to NEVER ignore red flags and NEVER make excuses for anyone. Most importantly if God isn't present make him present.

I believe the Lord was telling me to surrender in my marriage, but I kept fighting in a sense. I didn't want to be a failure and divorce. That was my mind frame at that time. I now know, I was supposed to just let go. I was there to learn about me, from him as well as from myself in the process. I was also there to teach and shed light. I believe God places us where we need to be, to help us grow or to teach. Sometimes we just don't know when it's time to walk away.

God showed me a lot in this relationship/marriage. I learned more about myself in this relationship than I ever learned in any relationship. I'm not sure if I was more receptive and introspective, but learned a great deal and I cherish that growth. I needed to grow in how I communicate in frustration, whether it's to lash back or stay silent, which I did both. I also learned that sometimes you cannot love someone how they want you to love them. Some love has to come from their parents, family, friends, or more importantly GOD. You can't replace a love you've yearned for, from your mate. That void will never get filled. You will drive yourself crazy trying to "prove your love". I also learned that grown folks are going to do what grown folks are going to do and you have no control of another person's thoughts, actions or feelings.

My biggest lesson was magnified through my best friend. Here's the thing. I have been proposed to a few times, I've said no and I've said yes. My best friend of many years told me, that I allow the guy to guide me down the aisle in a sense. In other words, they run with the "let's get married or have a relationship" and I go along with it. She also said I don't lead the thought. My friend is absolutely right! That was an issue with me, but not anymore. With God, I am the captain of my ship. I have learned not to make any decision without speaking to God first and foremost. I now ask God to reveal what He needs to reveal to me and allow me to see things clearly. That is extremely important! Am I now dating? Yes I am. Would I get married again? I would love to marry again, but only if it's right! I am a hopeless romantic, so sometimes things can get a little cloudy. I will pray and talk to God first because He has the final say.

There is a price to pay. The most difficult part of this experience was me labeling myself a big fat failure. I cried for months when we divorced. I was sad, hurt, angry, confused and disappointed at the resolution of our marriage. Although I knew we shouldn't have gotten married, I still didn't want to admit to the failure. I remember not telling anyone, but my best friend and my mother that it was over. I would run into people that attended our wedding and they would ask about "us" and I never told them we split, out of being embarrassed and ashamed. I felt like I let people down. I went through it emotionally for months.

If I could change the chain of events, I would have waited to get married. I would have read all the signs and knocked down all the red flag issues. What glitters in the beginning isn't always gold. Sometimes it's brass and that tarnishes, if not polished regularly. God would have been the polish that made us shine.

I truly believe that you should not get married until you truly love yourself. It may be a cliché but it is so very true. You can't give someone you, if you haven't learned to love and accept yourself for who you really are. You have to come face to face with your past and address issues you have and be content with the present. When people say, "I want a man/woman who completes me." I get so mad at that statement because it's the biggest and wackiest statement ever said. You don't need anyone to complete you. You need to be a complete person when you enter a marriage and so does your mate. 100% and 100%, not 50%-50%, THAT WILL NEVER WORK. Marriage is already difficult, but if you start off as only a half person, you are preparing for disaster and heartbreak. You need whatever void filled before you enter a marriage. God is in the business of filling voids. "Got God?"

Real conversations with your mate are a must before you get married. You have to be on the same page with your short term and long term goals. People often grow apart because they

Dear Lord, I Think I Married The Wrong Person

didn't have a conversation pass the present. You have to dig deep about goals, finances, future career goals, family, insurance, death, vacations, relocations, ex-spouses, children(current and potential), friends, business, to rent or own a home... etc. You can never assume that someone else wants what you want. You cannot marry someone just because you "love" them. It has to be much more. That's what will sustain your marriage when the love is a little shaky.

    I think you have to genuinely like the person and be real friends before walking down that aisle. Marriage is about love, but as I get older I've learned it's about business also. That "madly in love," phase may not last. You may have days where you aren't feeling the love. That doesn't mean go or flee the relationship. It just means you focus on the other things about your mate that you like until the love resurfaces. Now, if you don't have anything else, then what? That's why it's important to pay attention to everything else you like about the person. If you only bet on love, you will lose every time in a marriage. As Mary J. Blige sang, *It Ain't All Roses* There are good and bad days, but you have to have what it takes to get through the not so good days.

    God is able to change or fix anything. All you have to do is call on Him. God also helps those who help themselves. "Faith without works is dead" (James 2:26). You have to do the work before you get married and you have to put in the work to have a happy, loving and healthy marriage. I believe in marriage and I believe marriage does work. I would love to have a healthy, happy, and successful marriage. I, just like anyone, have to be willing to put in the work and my mate would have to do the same.

I would suggest to everyone to do your homework and never settle for less than you are worth. That goes for the ladies and the gentlemen. Every one of God's children is special and deserves nothing less than the best. Don't accept anyone into your life that doesn't truly want the best for you and doesn't recognize the best in you. We all deserve to be loved but that love starts with you. You have to love yourself as God loves you. Once you conquer that beautiful concept then the flood gates will open for you to find your special lifelong love.

This is My Story: I just wanted to make some things clear. These are my feelings and thoughts. This is not in any way, anything to disrespect anyone especially my ex. All relationships start off one way and sometimes for whatever reason end in a different way. Just because my ex was not for me doesn't mean he's a bad guy, because he isn't by any means. He's actually a great guy. All of our time together was not bad. He was good to me too and I cherish and remember those moments, just the same. I want my ex to be blessed in abundance!

Years after the divorce and not seeing each other, he invited me for sushi. We had a good time! There were some tears as well as laughter. We spoke about our friendship and former marriage. We got some things out that needed to be said and we communicated like old friends, like we were many, many years ago. We even spoke about present relationships and what we've learned and what we took from each other. It was very touching.

Dear Lord, I Think I Married The Wrong Person

I say all that to say, just because mistakes are made and divorces are finalized doesn't mean you can't come back together to make your peace. It's a beautiful thing, if you are adult enough to do that. We are all God's children and we all are worthy of forgiveness and love. It's in all of us.

All things are pieces of fabric that's added to the quilts that is our lives. Our experiences make us who we are.

~Kendell Lenice

Dear Lord, I Think I Married The Wrong Person

Love

Love is special; it comes from God
We are born with it and of it
It truly exist
Sometimes we forget
Or listen to people; who don't seem to get it
How special you are
They then begin to leave scars
With words that are unkind
You begin to doubt the word love
But our love doesn't come from man
It comes from up above.
Man didn't make you
And should never break you
Seek God
And you'll find the answer

By,
Kendell Lenice

Dear Lord, I Think I Married The Wrong Person

Prophetess Amanda Williams

is a prolific author, conference host and inspirational speaker. It is evident that the power of God is using this woman through the manifestation of signs and wonders. Lives are being changed by the cutting edge approach to the Word of God exemplified in the domestically held conferences yearly. She is known by her tenacity and her boldness of preaching as she rightly divides The Word of God, while being used prophetically. She will give The Body precisely as God gives it to her, holding nothing back and in return, she is given the honor of seeing lives changed everywhere The Holy Spirit allows her to minister.

God has given Prophetess Amanda Williams a prophetic voice, causing her to be precise as she delivers prophetically. She operates in the gifts of discernment, faith, healing, miracles and prophecy. In her many conferences, testimonies are in abundance; of souls saved, lives restored, and bodies healed. She is a much sought after speaker who is no stranger to pain and suffering, and she is the author of the book, *I Survived*.

Prophetess Amanda Williams is the mother of three children, Jonathon, Brandon and Bianca, all of which are college graduates. She is a Business graduate, and her motto is, *"You can only be it, if you can believe it."* She is a woman who is fulfilling the clarion call of God and knows that with God, there are no limitations; nothing shall be impossible to them that believe.

The ministry website is: www.amandawilliams.us or you may email her at: amw4069@yahoo.com.

In Spite of It All I Made It

Marriage is a union that is meant to be shared between a man and a woman, and with the right ingredients it can last a lifetime. Although I have endured pain in marriage and suffered through many trials, marriage is a beautiful thing, and I will never allow a bad situation to hinder a good thing. Marriage was ordained by God and meant to be sacred.

When young girls grow up without the loving nurture of a father they feel the need to be loved and as they get older they usually start looking for love in the wrong places; and, oftentimes they get it from the wrong people. A young woman's desire for love is natural because love is a part of her being, but if she hasn't been given love or taught its attributes, she really doesn't know what to accept or what to look for. That is how most young ladies become open prey for men, at an early age.

I was pregnant at the age of fifteen but I knew that I would be fine because from an early age I had a strong belief, your journey will be as *you* destine and circumstances do not dictate your outcome unless you allow them too. You can overcome and you can achieve.

My son indeed was a blessing. But, I had no idea that the road ahead would be filled with bad decisions, abuse, pain and suffering. And due to my choices, I'd experience betrayal by the very ones that I thought loved me, and left with wounds that only God could heal, and I thank Him that He did heal.

Dear Lord, I Think I Married The Wrong Person

No matter what you have to go through in life, whether it's because of the choices you made, or whether you suffered at the hands of someone else's negligence, you can still come out *victoriously*. I now know that my journey was all a part of God's plan for my life because He said that *all things worketh together for the good to them that love the Lord and are the called according to His purpose*. Maybe not the way it all happened was His will, but He has a way of making it all work out for you.

I believe that it had to happen in order for me to become the woman that I am today, a woman who teaches other young women to love themselves, educate themselves and that a man should be a complement, not a necessity.

There are many women that will never experience marriage (because of their own personal preference), but whatever the case may be, they are at peace and that's what matters. It doesn't matter where destiny takes you, but what matters is that you live a happy, enriched, prosperous, and satisfying life.

Just as there are single women who may not get married again, or never experience marriage, there are also women that are married and miserable; they wear masks to hide the pain and feel they have to stay for the sake of either, people, (worried about what people will say if they leave), or circumstances (in most cases, financial reasons – afraid that they can't do it on their own). They don't realize that it is wrong and unfair to both parties to stay in a miserable situation.

Last, but not least, there are those that are married and loving every moment of it; they are happy, and that is because they are with their soul mate (I've written a poem at the end of this chapter titled, *My Soulmate*, just for them). When you are connected with the one that God gave you, there's nothing that you can't work out or work through because love is the force behind the relationship, and love is power. Love brings joy. I personally would rather have a broke man that loves me and can build with me, than a man with riches, who doesn't love me, but is capable of giving me the world on a silver platter.

As Christians, we have mastered how to make things LOOK LIKE it's of God…even marriages. It's funny how when we get married we tend to say this is the mate that God sent me. But, if it ends in divorce, we'll say the devil sent him/her. What God joined together, let no man put asunder; but let's keep it real, God doesn't join all marriages together. In fact, He sometimes says "NO", in the first place, but we do it anyway, and that is the **primary** reason it don't last. You do know that if God can create a man/woman, He can surely hold a marriage together.

I am so thankful that what the devil thought was defeat for me, has actually been my greatest triumph, and that is why I am able to share my story with you. My prayer is that as you read the chapters in this book, that you will be healed, delivered and live life at the fullest intent, without shame or regret, and without looking back. Whoever has left you, was supposed to leave. And, if what we've endured will help you not to make the same mistakes, or travel similar paths, then our journey has paid off, in full.

This was not my first marriage, but I thought there was nothing greater than to be joined together with a saved man. I *thought* that because we were both Christians, this was finally it, and to me, there was nothing sweeter than two people together, who love God. After all, saved folk surely should be the ones who know how to work through obstacles, and if anybody can stay together, it ought to be Christians. But, of course, it didn't work out that way.

When I came out of that marriage, I came out knowing that I'd rather have an unsaved man any day, who doesn't know, than to have a saved one, who does know, but doesn't do; I didn't know which case was worse, but I thanked God for bringing me out of it!

I met him one day while I was leaving a place of business. When I met him, The Lord told me that he would ask me to go out to dinner. *I thought* it'd be that weekend, but it was about a week later. I wasn't certain that I wanted to go out to dinner with him because at that time I was healing from a previous relationship and I wasn't that interested in seeing anyone. But when he asked, I decided to go ahead and go, and maybe going would help me to do better at moving forward. After all he was a saved man and I'd become weary of meeting my preference so what better man than God's man?

I can remember it as though it was yesterday. He picked me up on a Friday evening and off to dinner we went. At first, I wasn't having a good time because of course my heart was somewhere else (just being honest) but he was actually kind of funny so I began to be at ease. We laughed, talked, and ultimately enjoyed the evening. It was good for me because it was just clean laughter and great conversation. BUT on our way back, he started talking about MARRIAGE and how he'd been on his knees praying for a godly wife, etc. I was thinking to myself NO way!

He later said to me that God told him that I was his wife. Somehow, I wanted to believe him, and I guess eventually I did believe him. I prayed about it and to this day, I believe that God sent me into his life because he had prayed for a godly wife. We are divorced now, and I am at peace with it all because I know that I did what was required of me. God can bless you with something (someone), but if you're not careful, you can forfeit your own blessing(s).

It's better to marry than to burn; this is true, but it's much better to pray that you be kept, and what needs to be taught in the church is restraint. To ask The Lord to keep you while He's preparing your mate for you, and help you enjoy your life until that time comes! Many are falling into the deception that you have to be married to be holy, but the truth is that you need to be holy to be married.

The church teaches that dating is sin, but there's nothing wrong with dating; there's something wrong with having sex while dating! Nowadays, folk are getting married in a hurry, to live right, but they should live right…then, get married. And by all means, get to know the person that you are planning to spend the rest of your life with!

MAKE SURE it's of God because that's the only way it's going to last. That's why most get married three or four times before they actually marry the right person, but to be honest, it shouldn't take that many times before you find Mr. or Mrs. Right.

Dear Lord, I Think I Married The Wrong Person

To make a long story short, I dated him a short while, praying that I wouldn't turn down a man that (I believed) God had sent me. I got a phone call one day, and it was my cousin (who was more like a sister to me). She told me that she had a dream the night before, and in her dream, I was getting ready to get married. She gave me detailed information, and keep in mind, I hadn't discussed anything with her because up unto that point, I really wasn't sure about marrying him. I was waiting on a sign from God, and when I received that call, you know I believed that was a sign from God. On top of that, another woman I knew in my hometown called me and told me that she'd had a dream and it was so similar to the one that my cousin had previously had. It was then, that I just *knew* that I was to marry him. So I did.

Boy oh boy! A week into the marriage, and I felt that I'd been seriously betrayed, and this was something that I wouldn't want any other woman to have to go through – it was an assignment against me, my ministry and my integrity.

Although I have no regrets now, due to the fact that, *In Spite of It All, I Made It,* I endured painful betrayal. It left me asking, WHY? I guess because when I met him, I wasn't seeking a husband, nor was I really interested in him (I had sought God concerning him BEFORE I said I do). And this time, I honestly believed it would be different because both of us were Christians.

I came out of that relationship pleading for a heart of forgiveness and that I wouldn't harbor bitterness in my heart towards him. I knew that if I didn't truly forgive him, I would hinder and ultimately stop my own blessings. I wasn't willing to allow anyone that type of control over me.

Dear Lord, I Think I Married The Wrong Person

I can truly say that by the time of the divorce, I was **completely** healed, totally restored and I'd honestly forgiven him for what he'd done. No, I wasn't perfect, but I didn't do anything that would lead to a divorce.

Why did the marriage have to happen? I don't really know but maybe God wanted to teach me some things as well as for him to see that He could have a godly wife, as he'd been praying for, and yet maybe a godly wife wasn't what he truly wanted. I must admit though, even through the betrayal (*some of you are wondering what was it*...but I think you are smart enough to figure it out), I was blessed because I learned so much from it; I call it Life's Lessons. I am a believer that if you learn from a bad situation, it is never defeat.

WARNING! To those of you that are praying for a spouse: be careful because the devil knows what you are praying for, and he will oftentimes send false signs and counterfeits. This is to keep you from your true blessing (mate). All the signs may appear to be from God, but you better make sure because your salvation is at stake. God will never send you a man/woman that you have to constantly worry about, or one that's going to take you out of His will. The person that God gives to you will love you unconditionally-NO strings attached, and your provision, concern and livelihood will matter the most. *The devil is a trickster*. He knows what you want and he'll dress someone up just for you but his only plan is to use *that* person to take you out of the will of God.

I was married to him a little over two years (really amazed that it lasted that long). The battle seemed like it had been a lifetime, but the blessings were well worth the wait. You see, I was on fire for God, and the devil THOUGHT he was going to use that marriage to put my fire out...BUT, the devil was a LIAR, and he IS a LIAR! Before that marriage, I could never really talk about betrayal. So now when I tell a person that you can overcome the worst form of betrayal, it's because I truly overcame and I KNOW that ALL THINGS worketh together for the good to them that love the Lord and are the called according to His purpose! Your greatest testimony is the one that you experience personally.

I am a firm believer that there are always warning signs (even with that); we just overlook them. See with your spirit, not with your natural eyes or you'll definitely miss the warnings. They're always there. All of my life, I've wanted a man who would love me...plain and simple, and the devil knew that.

Since I've been a Christian; all I've wanted was a man who truly loves God...what better man to send me. After all, I had no faith in a man that didn't go to church. But now I wonder and I don't know which is worse, one that go to church and should do better or one that don't go to church and don't know better. One thing I do know, *and that is*, the next time, I WILL KNOW!

You may be saying, the next time? Yes, **I will get married again.** I just know. *In Spite of It All*, I believe in marriage, and I'll never give up on love. The things I've had to go through have all taught me the value of the anointing, and my own self-worth. I understand that *when you are anointed, you have to be careful*. You have to guard your anointing because the devil will send his greatest chiefs after you.

Dear Lord, I Think I Married The Wrong Person

Let me help you get free right now; folk that are looking for a reason to stone you, will stone you anyway, so if you are staying in a bad marriage for the sake of folk...you'll stay miserable. What they say, think or feel about you does not matter. I am a much better woman now and I believe it's because I don't care what the people think, feel, or say. When you've gone through as much as I've endured I guess letting go is one of your trademarks; what doesn't kill you can only make you stronger.

I have much compassion for young women; I have a daughter and I have done my best to teach her about life. She knows the value of being independent because I've taught her to be. I realize that many young ladies now often meet a "sugar daddy" along the way, whether they're eighteen or thirty, and if not they're not careful, he becomes "daddy" – a controller. Sugar daddies control you with money and the lavishness of life, but it often ends in abuse and sometimes death. If a young lady knows how to take care of herself more than likely she won't turn to a sugar daddy. Love yourself and never settle for less than God's best for you. You don't have to settle for just *any* man. Self-value will last a lifetime. Stop looking for love in all the wrong places and look for it from within.

Each of us have our own personal journey that we must take, and some take longer than others but ultimately we'll end up at the same place if we don't faint (give up). The road bumps along the way are not meant to stop us but they do sometimes make the journey rougher (those are called lessons).

If I had one thing that I could change about my life, I do know that I would be more careful in making decisions. However,

Dear Lord, I Think I Married The Wrong Person

I also realize that if I'd done anything differently, I know that I wouldn't be who I am now; therefore, I can't really say that if I could change one single thing, what that one thing would be. If I had the power to change anything, I wouldn't be me, and I LOVE ME.

I am at my best place in life right now. I am living my best life now. I am free; I am happy. I am living my life the way God has purposed it. I have three wonderful children (all of which are now adults – gone and grown) and by the way that child that I had when I was fifteen, graduated from college with a Ph.D. God is good!! I told you that ALL things worketh together…

I enjoy life, and I love seeing lives changed by the power of God and people living the abundant life that Christ came to give. There are two important things I need for you to know about change. Change is often difficult. Going from being married to becoming single was change for me but I can truly say that it's not as bad as some folk make it sound and I will enjoy it while I can; right now it's just me and God, and it's wonderful. Also, change means to turn around and yes you do have the power to change your situation today. Although I look forward to marriage again someday; I enjoy being single right now. I have no regrets of a bad marriage, but I look forward to a good one (in God's timing).

In closing, I pray that you will experience the true meaning of love, first of all, within yourself. Know that marriage is not just an emotional act. Those of you that are married, I pray that you will experience its overflow of joy, love, peace and unity. And to those that have been hurt in a relationship; release the hurt and bitterness so that when your mate does come, you'll be ready.

Dear Lord, I Think I Married The Wrong Person

Make sure that you heal completely BEFORE you go into another commitment, or you will never be able to enjoy the fullness of the relationship. Whatever you do, **enjoy life**...with or without a mate and be the best you that you can be!

Dress up, look good for yourself and if you are married or dating, look good for him. Remember, Jezebel still lurks and if you won't, she will. Don't you give up hope; you will have what you believe. Married or single, set goals for yourself. Take charge over your own life. Dare to believe. Your past is what shaped your future; and whatever you do, do not despise it. *In Spite of It All*, God made it all work out for you. You are still here!

Divorce is definitely not a good thing, but it's not the end of the world. I do believe that the church needs to speak up and properly educate both singles and married folk on relationships; it's time for the church to come out of the closet and through the proper education, help bring the statistics down on the divorce rate. If we pull together we can possibly put an end to the divorce climate. By being honest and with the proper education, I believe that people will be more careful before saying I do and those that say it will take marriage more seriously.

If you are married and having problems, that doesn't mean go get a divorce. I realize that sometimes divorce is the answer, but in most cases it is not. Whatever you do make sure you've done what The Lord required of you before you exit. I do not encourage anyone to live in a harmful situation or to live unhappily, but neither do I support divorce. Only you and God can make the decision. With Him you can and you will make the right decision.

Dear Lord, I Think I Married The Wrong Person

I pray healing over all those that read this book.

I have written the following poems just for you, to give you hope and confidence along the way. Enjoy and God bless you.

Signed,

Amanda Williams
A friend of marriage and an enemy of divorce

Dear Lord, I Think I Married The Wrong Person

My Soulmate

When you meet your soulmate you will know,
there's something within that tells you so.
An inner peace comes over you,
letting you know this one is true.
Spirits will connect from deeply within,
By this you'll know, you've found your "friend".
In case you're wondering how do I know
When I met you, I found half my soul.
If there was a day for soul mates to be
It'd be specially designed for you and for me.
Rain, sunshine, sleet nor snow
Can never hinder our passionate flow.
because I know we were meant to be
Soulmates for life-yes, you and me.

Amanda Williams

Dear Lord, I Think I Married The Wrong Person

Trust God

Trusting in man is not wise to do
There are times in life man will fail you.
With you today, though tomorrow may not
Change like the weather-from cold to hot.

Life can make you or break you they say,
But when you trust God, He makes it ok.
Though meant for bad, it still worked for you
That's what Trusting in God will do.

You reap what you sow, so sow good seed
and, do what you can to keep the peace.
Believe in Him, although you can't see
And, your life will be filled with joy and peace.

Amanda Williams

Dear Lord, I Think I Married The Wrong Person

Prophetess Tracy Davis

was born and raised in Cleveland, Ohio to Alvin and Lizzie Tucker whom she loves dearly. Raised from a newborn as a Muslim in the Nation of Islam, her Dad was and still is a devout Muslim and her Mom followed him for years (even though she was a Christian at heart). Deliverance came to her mother and spread throughout her children like wildfire converting them to the true Word of God!

Prophetess Davis makes special appearances on Simple Words Ministry which is under the leadership of Pastor Maureen Chen.

She is the proud mother of six beautiful children (five boys and one girl). She effectively balances motherhood and ministry with ease and excellence. She has one book presently published entitled, *Come out of the Cocoon* and she is currently working on her second piece to a literary series God is using her to birth out.

She resides in Cleveland, Ohio with her beautiful family.

Check out her website at:
www.cutfromthesameclothministries.com

Dear Lord, I Think I Married The Wrong Person

The Love of Jesus Brought Me Out

And Gave Me something to Shout About

The Bible declares in 2 Corinthians 6:14, *Be ye not unequally yoked together with unbelievers: for what fellowship hath righteousness? And what communion hath light with darkness?* A powerful scripture indeed and frequently overlooked.

Emotions can cause you to make some harmful decisions. What looks good on the outside, to the natural eye, may not be good for you. The heart must always be guarded. Proverbs 4:23, *keep thy heart with all diligence; for out of it are the issues of life.* The New Living Translation says it this way, *Guard your heart above all else, for it determines the course of your life.* Basing decisions on how we feel is dangerous. I've learned to base all decisions on what God says for me to do, even in matters of the heart.

Marriage is an awesome union when its partakers have put God in front. God must be the head of the marriage; forever above the husband and wife. If He is not the head, the foundations will crumble. I know this now but my heart blocked out what God was yelling at me to understand. I have been married twice. I have had one divorce and am going through another at this very moment. It is in the second marriage that I realized how important it was to be spiritually in tune with GOD and to not totally rely on emotion.

Dear Lord, I Think I Married The Wrong Person

I was born and raised a Muslim. When I met my first husband we both were into that religion. My father was a Muslim to the core and still is, my mom was a Christian at heart. However, she yielded to her husband as he was the head of house. One day my mom decided she didn't want to be here anymore. She didn't want to go through her marriage anymore and so she decided to commit suicide due to all the pain that my father had caused her. My sister found her, pills on her chest, lying on the stairs barely alive.

They rushed her to the hospital and she did make it through. Shortly after, her brother called her to go to church and she accepted. She fell into Jesus' arms and she never looked back. I, however, remained a Muslim; A child which grew up into a hateful adult. My foundation was formed and set on destructive relationships.

I met my first husband while working in an assisted living facility. Our relationship was beautiful in the beginning. We dated about a year before I had my first child when I was nineteen, my second when I was twenty and my third at twenty-one. Shortly after the birth of my third child, we got married.

When I met him I knew nothing about Jesus. My God was Allah and that is all I knew. We constantly fought. He laid around all day smoking marijuana and drinking beer. Although I had a full scholarship for accounting. I began to sink into depression.

I got on welfare, started partying, drinking, smoking, clubbing, and I left my first two children behind with my mother in-law. Sadly, I missed the first few years of my children's lives. My husband began to hang out over his friend's house.

It was after my third child was hospitalized, dehydrating, and dying, that I had my Damascus Road experience. Allah couldn't help me. I knew to call out to my mom. I praise God for a praying mother. She came to the hospital and prayed for him. Speaking in tongues, rubbing his body, holding him tightly as she prayed, it wasn't long before I saw my son's color come back into his face, tears returned, and he looked up at her and smiled. He drank bottle after bottle of Pedialyte to rehydrate himself.

I felt a warm presence and I desired to have what she had. My son's life was saved by someone and I wanted to know this being they called Jesus.

After that dreadful yet miraculous experience, I went to church with my mom and I got filled with the Holy Spirit in the middle of service. The reason I married my husband at this time was because I was told I had to marry him or I couldn't get baptized. An older woman at the church stated this. I felt I wanted Jesus so bad, even though I knew I shouldn't marry him, I did it to be baptized.

I began to work as a State Tested Nursing Assistant on the graveyard shift while he stayed at home with the children. I could feel myself begin to lose all respect for him. I begged him to get up and help me take care of the children. It never happened.

The marriage went completely downhill after this. Arguments turned into fist fights. This went on for ten long years and six kids later. I had a nervous breakdown. I went to a

Dear Lord, I Think I Married The Wrong Person

psychiatrist and they prescribed pills, I got on disability and was literally a wreck for years. I know it was my mom praying for me that finally brought me through. *I could feel a calling on my life but just couldn't get up to do a thing about it.*

One year I decided to get up and go back to school. This time I got a Medical Assistant license and began to work at a hospital. I had begun to smoke cigarettes again and had an occasional drink. Here is where I met husband number two. He was a delivery man for the hospital I worked for. He asked me out and because I was so sick of my marriage and was waiting to file divorce, I agreed.

Please be careful of wolves in sheep clothing. He said all the right things, gave me money to help pay my bills, and even took interest in my children. I got a divorce and he held my hand through it. The thing about it is; I couldn't see all the problems emerging early on because we both were drinking and partying. I gave up my home to move in with him and that's when the relationship changed. The foundation we started this relationship on was very rocky.

His family came against me because I was 28 years old and had six children. They couldn't understand what he wanted with me. I was in a backslidden condition because I'd let the hurt from my first marriage scar me so much. We argued and fought. I spit on him, he head butted me, and I called the police. These are just some of the things that took place *before* this marriage. Once again my heart said, "Marry him anyway, everything will get better once you get married." So we married August 1, 2009.

Dear Lord, I Think I Married The Wrong Person

Fights escalated and his family even came over to fight me. One day something devastating happened to my daughter and it made me return to GOD. The way I felt about it was I had two choices. Go back to God or go to jail for doing something to the person who hurt my daughter. I sat in a car, holding a knife, and the Lord told me to go back into the house. At that moment I rededicated my life to Christ and things got better in the home for a while.

After crossing that devastating situation, my marriage got back to the same turmoil it was before. I prayed, I cried, we separated, and we got back together. I asked GOD to give him a mind to want to serve Him. I could feel hatred rising in him towards me. I felt he didn't like me going to church. He never said it but he would bring it up when we argued. So, I stayed home more. I did everything to make sure he was okay. He had two children as well living with us. One was an autistic son of about 28 yrs. old. His daughter was around 7 yrs. old when I first met her

I felt he constantly put his daughter above my needs (as well as everybody else) and would flip out if I had anything to say about it. We were together for five years and married for two. It finally all boiled over and the last argument turned into a fight where we both ended up in jail. It was in jail as I ministered to other hurting women, that I finally understood the call on my life. I finally understood what God was trying to show me. I'll tell you what He was trying to show me in a moment.

When I got home from a half day in jail, God is good, me and my husband separated. I went through a series of feelings;

Dear Lord, I Think I Married The Wrong Person

Depression, anger, hurt, even suicide. He began to cut off all the utilities from me and my children. I was left with a rent and back rent too high for me to pay on my own. He turned off every phone in the house and the furniture was repossessed. He left me with no car to get around.

God is so faithful people! My dad fixed my car, a church gave me money to pay backed up rent, another church gave me food, my mom purchased clothes for my children, and many gave my children gifts for the Christmas tree. I praise GOD! I realize the call on my life is to help others to repentance. To introduce them to the King of Kings; the one who kept me through all of the things I have just shared with you. I am to preach the gospel of Christ to the broken that they might be mended. Praise GOD!

I may not have furniture in my home, may not have the best clothes, may not have the van I need to get around, may not have a phone or cable TV; what I do have is irreplaceable. I have God, my children, peace, joy, mercy and favor. I HAVE JESUS!

He taught me that there is nothing or no one on earth that will ever love me like He does. There is truly nobody like HIM. He taught me to trust in HIM, truly love HIM and myself. He taught me to not look at what I don't have but be grateful for what I do have. My children have their health and so do I, I have support from friends and family, and I HAVE JESUS!!!!!!!!! That is the greatest of them all. Furniture will come, clothes will come, van will come, cable will come, and phone service will come. Seeing my children happy again and getting hugs and kisses from them is priceless. My first book is *Come out of the Cocoon*, and that is exactly how I feel. I feel totally free as if I have come out of my own personal cocoon.

The moral is no matter what your heart feels it may not be what God wants for you. We must always be led by the spirit. It took fifteen years (ten years with husband one and five years with husband two) for me to learn this. God is our source, not man. I believe God has my Boaz somewhere out there and one day we will meet, but as for right now I am learning to be content in GOD. He is everything to me. I have faith that He will supply all of our needs.

I have no regrets and I wouldn't change a thing. I believe what I have been through has sculpted me into the person I am today. My prayer is never for God to remove me from the trials and tribulations, but instead to help me go through them. These trials have brought wisdom at a young age. I praise GOD that He has given me a testimony for someone else. I have learned patience, longsuffering, how to love, how to forgive, how to praise, how to worship, and how to stay on my knees in prayer.

I am currently still separated from my second husband and waiting on a divorce. I am working on book two entitled, *Armed & Dangerous*. I minister on Simple Words Ministry. I attend New Zion Gospel Church and I am leaving myself open to whatever it is the LORD will have me to do. I gave myself away to HIM. I believe God for many more ministering opportunities to share my story and the Word of God! Allow me to pray for you:

Dear Lord, I Think I Married The Wrong Person

My prayer for you dear children of God is

this; Father God, in the name of Jesus, I worship, honor and adore you. I ask that you touch every heart and begin to mend it, in Jesus name. I ask that you Lord will apply yourself to every battle scar upon them in the name of Jesus. I pray that you will continue to guide your children, ordering every step in Jesus Name. Mend broken hearts. Mend broken marriages if it be in your will. Help us to be sensitive to your voice and to your movements in Jesus Name. Lord God, send peace and strength to those going through divorces. Lord God let them know that you love them, you care for them, you see what they are going through, and that you are holding them in the palm of your hand. Let them know they can make it. Speak to them; rock them to sleep in the loneliness of night time, in Jesus name. We give you all the glory, honor and praise, in Jesus Name. Amen.

God has truly got each and every one of you in the palm of His hand. Trust in Him, lean on Him if you got to. He will never move so you can fall, He will hold you up. The joy of the Lord is truly your strength. Remember... wait on the Lord. God Bless you!

Kingdom Love to all,

Prophetess Tracy Davis

Update... After the completion of this short testimony, God has blown my mind again. I am adding this a month after its completion. I thought my story had ended but this proves to us once again that God is faithful. **My husband and I are fully reunited!** We have been drawn together all over again by GOD. Here is the next lesson and it is this:

It Ain't Over Until God Says It's Over!!!

Even though we were separated I continued to pray for my husband. Along with the prayers of others, God has brought him home. We are deeper in love than we ever were. God has reignited the flame that the enemy tried to snuff out. Through it all I have learned to be that Proverbs 31 woman. I know my role and stand by my husband against every attack. Sometimes saints, it takes a breaking to remove the faulty foundation that a marriage is built upon. It must be replaced with the solid rock. That rock is Jesus.

We have both found the errors of our ways and our love has become stronger than ever. These trials and tribulations have actually brought us closer together and have made us strong. Saints, I have my family back and God gets all the Honor and Glory!!!!!!!!!!! Hallelujah!!!!!!! God Bless each and every one of you.

Dear Lord, I Think I Married The Wrong Person

I am praying for each of your relationships. May God get the Glory and Honor in every situation in **Jesus Name**!!!!!!! Amen.

www.ingramcontent.com/pod-product-compliance
Lightning Source LLC
Chambersburg PA
CBHW060502090426
42735CB00011B/2085